Me A

*How the Guy Who Never Got Paid Much
Shocked the World by Retiring Early, and
How You Can Too!*

Dan P. Schaefer

Contents

INTRODUCTION

Facebook status update, prepared in advance and saved for posting on the day I publicly declared financial independence:

I've decided to take my life in a different direction.

Not so many years ago, I came up with an answer to the challenging question, "What do I want to be when I grow up?" My answer: Semi-Retired Singer, Songwriter, and Author. Getting from Point A (net worth close to zero, monthly expenses roughly equal to or slightly above monthly income, a sad 401k left unattended because I didn't even know the web address to check it much less the login password) to Point B (now) took planned sacrifice, hard work, and not just willingness but true desire to gain knowledge in fields like finance and self-psychology. I got there.

The job I've held for the last 18-plus years while surviving approximately 15 corporate downsizings ("Account Manager" for a well-run, respected distribution company in the entertainment field) has been rewarding, excessively challenging, fun, maddening, interesting, boring, exciting, overwhelming, enriching, death-hastening, and, in the end, simultaneously too much and not enough. I probably cared too much and got too good at my job, and it turned into something that nearly destroyed me. I sincerely love my coworkers (a truly incredible bunch of individuals) and boss (smart, fair, appropriately driven, and just a great guy). I feel like many of my customers (some of whom I've known for more than twenty years spent with two music and video distributors) are family. I'll miss daily interaction with these friends. But it's past time for me to do something else, not just because I can but because it's what my soul needs.

I'm semi-retiring as of today. Some of what I have planned will result in income going forward, but most incoming dollars will be the result of what I've already saved and put in places where it can now do the heavy lifting for me and flow back as passive income. Dave is choosing to continue to work at this time, and we'll reevaluate as life unfolds and we remain open to possibilities here and abroad. I could not be happier to say that we are both very much looking forward to the future.

If you're interested in knowing how I pulled off this trick, you may be glad to hear that I'm sharing my acquired knowledge and the strategies I created to achieve financial freedom on a modest income in just a handful of years. Interested in joining me, or perhaps in just reading way too many intimate details about my life? BUY THE BOOK! It's available now, e-book format only, on Amazon. $2.99.

Cheers!

Dan Schaefer
Semi-Retired Singer, Songwriter, and Author

I began composing my big, official announcement a few months earlier, moments after I decided to go ahead and pull the trigger. The circumstances surrounding these moments constitute an appropriate representation of how my entire plan worked from the start (and will continue to work for the rest of my life). You see, I made the decision to retire early on what many would consider a "shoestring" budget while floating in a luxurious private rooftop pool overlooking the Pacific. Oh, the gluttony! Oh, the self-pampering!

When we pull the camera back to expose more of the scene, we first see a beautifully-appointed patio with four seating areas, presently being enjoyed by just two guys who must think they're CEOs or something. How much is this costing?! Then we pull the camera back further and discover that the rooftop pool is a rather obvious outlier in a very low-income neighborhood well off the touristy strip in a resort town in Mexico, blocks from where most Americans might feel at ease. We're off-season and it's hot as hell. There's some sort of rooster breeding operation across the street, and the proud crowing of thirty or more of the things pretty much never stops. A handful of nefarious characters hang out on the steps outside the hopefully-secure entrance to the condo ("Hola, amigos!"). Very simple lives are being led three stories below on the streets of Puerto Vallarta, on the edge of *Zona Romantica*, where a middle-aged senora prepares tacos for the neighborhood every night and hombres gather on the sidewalk outside a small bar next door to watch soccer on a portable television. Garbage is piled high on the corner all the time, next to a sign that says something about it being illegal to put garbage there except on Tuesdays. Dirty kids play in the neighborhood at all hours, car engines backfire, marital arguments and festive parties fight for the honor of which is making the most noise. It's all in Spanish, and a bit overwhelming. But it's simple, and real, and because the dollar is very strong against the peso...it's really, really inexpensive. Thousands of Americans are vacationing in Destin or Panama City at the same moment, spending three times as much for a tiny balcony and a pool full of peeing kids.

We zoom back in to my smiling face in the rooftop pool. I'm kind of glowing at this moment, as the background noise fades. Because I'm in a freaking private rooftop pool overlooking the Pacific, and there's interesting stuff happening all around me, and this crazy luxury is costing less than a Red Roof Inn on the interstate in Tennessee because I did my research on the front end and was happy to compromise, and (best of all)...I've made a huge decision and it feels right and I won't have to sacrifice interesting, life-enhancing experiences in order to escape a life that was not working for me.

I found myself in this particular pool making this particular life decision after years of operating under a set of principles and strategies I created for myself, drawing from many others who have come before me and continue to provide valuable resources available to all of us thanks to the electronically connected nature of the world in which we now live. I started by identifying my problem (workplace stress threatening to kill me, and the feeling that I was living the wrong life) and deciding on a general and perhaps vague solution (get rid of the problem by stashing enough money to afford a life that feels right). I scoured web sites and talked to smart people and read books and more books, looking for a specific tried-and-true strategy that would work for me. In time, I realized that I'd need to combine a lot of *different* strategies in order to create a plan I could make stick, all the way to the end.

I'm kind of a casual guy, and I knew that if I tried to follow some sort of rigid, ultra-strict regimen I'd be doomed to fail. I also knew that I wouldn't mind sacrificing to reach my goal, but I didn't want to suffer. Life is short, and it can always end up being much shorter than we expect. I've experienced plenty of reminders of this! Debilitating health problems and surprise early deaths begin to surround us as we head into middle age. Had I keeled over dead before reaching the finish line, I'd have been pretty aggravated if I had denied myself all pleasure for years and years. A healthy compromise was possible, and achieved. I never wanted to lose sight of the many good things happening in my present as I tried to get to a better future. Sometimes I failed, and obsessed over nickels and dimes. But for the most part, I continued to live well as things progressed.

There are specifics to go with these generalities, and we'll get to them. Now that I'm on the other side of all this, it strikes me that the whole process was and is shockingly simple! It's kind of like floating down a river. Once you decide which river leads to the right lake or ocean and you get in your canoe, the current will take you in the right direction. You may occasionally need to avoid rocks or logs, or navigate dangerous rapids, but you can do that. If there's a fork in the river, you may need to decide which route to your destination will be better. You can do that too, knowing that you'll get there either way. Importantly, the river has always run in the same direction and will continue to do so. If you're happy on the shore, you can continue to sit there and enjoy yourself. But if you don't like your current spot, by all means...get in the canoe!

So let's dig into the details. First, we can look at what for a lot of us becomes a problem: the work-until-you're-dead American way of life. Then we'll check out how a growing number of us get out of the trap and into something nicer without going crazy first, concentrating on methods that have worked for one particular person (me). We start by saving and accumulating some money while we're stuck working for The Man, because he's the one who has the money. Then we gradually put that money to work on our behalf so it can turn itself into more money while we continue to save more and add to our stockpile. And finally, we reach a point at which our momentum is unstoppable, and since we no longer really need to keep adding more to the pile we declare ourselves financially independent from The Man and bid him a fond farewell.

Let's do this!

THE PROBLEM: WORKING TENDS TO SUCK (THE LIFE OUT OF A GUY)

From the outside, my job probably looked pretty cool. I got to work in the music and video industry, selling CDs and DVDs and vinyl records (and some other associated stuff) to retailers. Sometimes this involved me receiving free music and movies in the mail, and getting to go to free shows. (I was a buyer and marketing manager for a chain of record stores previously, and that involved even more fun freebies.) Best of all, perhaps? I got to work out of my house for a decent and respectable boss who was a thousand miles away and often left me to my own devices. Shower when you feel like it? Go to work in shorts and no shoes? Commute up some stairs every morning instead of fighting traffic? Wow! Why the hell is this guy complaining?

From the inside, my job ended up not being so cool. A combination of downloading taking market share from CDs and the economic downturn and eventual near-collapse during the Bush/Cheney years took a heavy toll on independent music retailers. As customers went out of business, my division's sales staff shrank from 45 reps to 17. Year after year, we would sit by the phone on downsizing day, waiting to find out if we were on The List or not. If we made the cut, we'd be tasked with calling stores one-by-one to let them know that their rep and long-time mutual friend was out on the street, and hello I'm your new rep, nice to meet you and sorry for the circumstances. Those of us who remained saw our account lists and workload increase steadily while our commissions decreased more and more.

Then came the resurgence of vinyl. It was unexpected, happened with dramatic speed, and saved our jobs. Suddenly sales volume was doubling, tripling, quadrupling. A whole new set of questions and problems and issues came into the daily mix. LPs are heavy and to save shipping money we had to split our orders and beat a daily ground shipping cut-off, then beat our end-of-day cut-off for everything else. Some of us were attending to hundreds of accounts all day, every day, and of course the company had to add employees to take care of everything, right? Well...no. We're in the U.S.A., where the goal tends to be getting as few people as possible to do as much work as they can handle without dying, for as little money as is required to keep them from leaving. The company actually downsized a few more times, as those of us who survived got increasingly crushed under the weight of our responsibilities.

One rep left by choice when the stress became too much and he began to suffer serious health problems. I thought it might be the start of something, but it wasn't. The rest of us stayed, and absorbed his accounts. Two more reps got fired the following year. So sorry, your rep and long-time mutual friend is out on the street, and hello I'm your new rep, nice to meet you and sorry for the circumstances.

We went through several ownership changes. The company went public, then went private again. Benefits packages changed, usually not for the better. Each ownership change brought a new round of downsizing and more work, and for some reason not one more rep chose to leave. I think we all liked our jobs, even if for many of us they had become more than overwhelming. I always kind of liked most of what I did; it's just that there was so much of it burying me at all times. Importantly, I tended to never lay blame on the ownership of the company (except for one set of owners who were pretty awful but didn't last long) or on my bosses. I blamed the American system, and I think I laid blame in the correct place. If a company wants to thrive in our country, it usually has to be as lean as possible. Sure, a ridiculous percentage of the spoils go to the very top, and we were not an exception. But again, this is how things presently work in our country. I think it's awful, and I think it will need to change fairly soon if we're to avoid a real collapse of the system, and I know that it's ultimately why I've chosen to leave...but for now, it's the way things are.

Vinyl kept selling like crazy, and the commission-based portion of my income started to increase a bit. I was overloaded, but enjoyed being in the black every month for a change. I'd been slowly eating through some inheritance money for a few years, and fortunately saw my paychecks increasing modestly just in time for me to stay above water. I was working in our independent retail sales division, and perhaps because I liked my customers and sincerely cared about helping them do well, my numbers looked good compared to those posted by most of my peers. Perhaps I was a victim of my own success.

One day I got a call from the boss, and learned that they wanted me to throw a foot into our chain division, and work on setting up vinyl inventory at a larger account that had yet to start doing business with us. I had no idea how this would work or how I could possibly handle one more thing on my plate, but I said I'd give it a shot. Things moved quickly, and their business shot through the roof. I liked my contacts at this big account very much, even in a *meet your new friend who will be like a little sister to you* sort of way, but the new situation was unbelievably intense and pressure-packed. I would have needed a staff of several employees working like dogs to cover the account in what I felt was an appropriate way, yet I was tasked with setting up my own procedures and handling a million new responsibilities and pressures at my house, by myself, feeling completely alone at almost all times. Overall, my combined indie and chain billing doubled, then tripled.

My health began to suffer considerably. I moved a million miles a second, every second of every day, experiencing shortness of breath, dizziness, blurred vision, fatigue, abdominal spasms, and chest pains. I took to keeping my cell phone at my side and leaving my front door open in case I needed to call the paramedics. I mentioned this to my boss and I'm pretty sure he thought I was joking or exaggerating. I paid a visit to the doctor (pretty unusual for me) for some tests, and was told that I was probably okay in the short term, but would need to address my work-related stress lest I die before too much time passed. I rushed back to work so I could beat the ground cut-off that day.

Things got worse. I would lie awake for hours thinking about work. Then I'd sleep for an hour or two before waking from nightmares about work, and lie awake for more hours thinking about my situation. The alarm would go off in the morning, and I'd wake literally screaming, "NO! I QUIT! NO! I CAN'T GO BACK UP THERE!" Then I would get to my desk and dig into hundreds of email messages and voice mail messages and a pile of tasks left on the back burner from the previous days, weeks, and months, and do my best to keep a cheery tone in my voice when the phone rang non-stop.

I all but stopped writing, recording, and performing my original music. It's what I moved to Nashville to do, and even through the worst of my day job misadventures I continued to create a bit here and there, but obviously I fell into a bit of a hole and let myself become overtaken by day-to-day stress. My relationship began to suffer, but thank goodness I had a supportive partner to help me survive. Along with everyone in my core group of friends, he begged me to quit and worry about the details later. But I didn't. I stuck it out, because I had come up with a plan.

I didn't want a short-term solution. Even more than I blamed American corporate culture for where I found myself, I blamed me. I figured that if I changed jobs, I'd probably find myself right back in a similar situation: overworked, unable to turn off the *I want to do my job extremely well* voice in my head, living the wrong kind of life, heading for a heart attack and/or stroke and/or early death. I wanted a permanent solution. And I made it my obsession to find one. Actually, I had already found it and had been quietly, casually taking steps on the road to a better place. It was just going to take some time for me to get there.

Late one night, early in the odyssey that became my most difficult working years, I was sitting on the sofa after Dave had gone to bed and I started randomly googling questions of desperation. I don't remember what all of the questions were, but I recall that one of them that started leading me in a productive direction was, "How can I retire on x-number of dollars?" I had casually begun to reduce my spending as my income had increased a little, and began to wonder if I might be on a good track. What if I kept going? Are there ways to escape this situation before it gets too much worse? I would fantasize about how much cash I might be able to save over random periods, then plug in dollar amounts and google my question. I was shocked to see so many answers on the internet!

I started clicking on articles and blogs and web sites. So many people had asked the same questions I was asking, and some had found answers! I didn't have much money at the time, so at first it looked like my only option would be to move Dave to the slums of India and live without electricity or water. Even I wasn't thrilled with that idea, but I started learning more about overseas retirement and it became my new favorite subject (more on that much later in this book). It seemed that thousands of Americans had found themselves in situations similar to mine, and for some of them an escape to a country with lower living costs had been the solution.

It was great to see that some of these escapees had figured out how to get out of the rat race having never had a super-high income. This gave me hope. One night I was sifting through success stories and asked myself out loud, "How are they doing this? How did they come up with enough money?" Gradually I determined that the answer involved some steps. First, start saving more. How? *I don't know, but I'll look into that later.* (It turns out that this is the most important step, and it's really not that complicated.) Second, take the savings and make that money turn itself into more money. How? *I don't know, but I'll look into that later.* (It turns out that this is the other most important step, and while it's a little more complicated it's really a lot easier than I ever dreamed.) Third, come up with the courage to get out of the chains and get the hell out of the standard American life timeline.

And so, I got started slowly and picked up the pace as I learned more. We're not planning to move to another country at this time, but my plan got us to a point at which we could do so and live comfortably in one of many acceptable locations. And we could do this now, if we decided it was what we wanted to do. It will cost more for us to stay here, largely because as we age our health care costs are likely to be higher here than anywhere else until our country musters the political will to fix a massive problem. But for now, we're staying put and planning to live on one income and two growing investment accounts as we see what develops and where life takes us. We're not sure how seriously we want to consider relocating, but at the very least the idea led to some really great fact-finding vacations and the discovery of methods that led me to financial independence.

It took some real effort (and several years of saying it over and over) for Dave to convince me that he not only wouldn't mind continuing to work while I jump out a little early, but that he would strongly prefer to do this. We both know that if it were solely up to me we probably would have retired to Costa Rica a while back, and one of the big reasons we're not there or in Mexico is that we want to remain close to Dave's parents, who are a car ride away and in their eighties. (I know from experience that this is important, having lost both parents, knowing I'll always treasure each moment

I was able to spend with them.) I got started on the program earlier and still invest more aggressively, so I guess I eventually decided it was okay to take advantage of my head start and constant attention to what the money is doing.

I really cannot wait to continue fine-tuning our investments while the passive income flows, while I also create and release music and perform live, and write and publish fiction and non-fiction that's been stuck in my head for years, and clear the basement of long-stored collectibles that will fly out of the house when I list them on eBay, and occasionally travel to new and interesting places on a budget. But enough about me and my plans. Let's talk about how I made all of this relaxed happiness a possibility, and see if perhaps you, too, can find your path to a better way of life.

THE SOLUTION, PART 1: SAVING

The goal, of course, is to end up with more money than you'll need to fund the rest of your life without having to deal with a bunch of daily crap in return for a paycheck. Because of the way money works in our slowly-recovering economy (and the way money works in most or all capitalist economies, really), saving a little from each check and plopping it into a checking account or a savings account earning interest way below the rate of inflation is simply not going to result in much progress. Saving alone is great, but the free market doesn't result in most of us getting paid enough to advance rapidly if we don't do something smart with the savings. Later, we'll look at how money, once saved, can be made to turn itself into more money and eventually into freedom.

Unless you're the head honcho at your workplace, you're stuck in a system designed to pay you enough to survive paycheck-to-paycheck and maybe, if you're careful and/or lucky, end up with a little extra you can save. Nobody is going to give you a bunch of extra money they don't have to give you, because they'd end up having to give a bunch of money to everyone else too and then they wouldn't be able to hoard all the money for themselves like head honchos do (and to some extent always have) in our society. But...nobody is forcing you to live your life the way most others at your income level are living theirs, considering many activities and products standard and necessary. A simple but important mindset shift can free up a huge amount of cash that, over time, has been quietly sneaking down the drain. We need this cash to stop disappearing so we can then do something great with it.

To get a bunch of bang out of our bucks, we must first come up with…a whole bunch of bucks. The more we save, the more we'll have to wisely, appropriately invest. And yes, I know. Right now a lot of you are thinking, "Save?! I can barely get by on what I make! What is this guy saying? This is stupid!" Stay with me! If you're getting by on an extremely meager income, your challenge will be a bit greater and you may need to think further "outside the box," and your progress may be more gradual. But that progress can be made at any income level. I'm here to tell you it doesn't take a massive income to get things rolling. I never made all that much money. I was fortunate to receive a bit of a windfall, an increase in the size of my paychecks, over my last few working years. But really, it wasn't much. I spent most of my working years on the low end of middle income, and probably snuck into "middle" middle income near the end.

I don't plan to go into specific dollar amounts regarding my past income. Partly, this is because former coworkers might end up reading this, and I don't think it's appropriate for me to divulge such specifics even if they all pretty much know what I made because most of us were on similar plans and because people talk. For instance, I know that toward the end I nudged my way up to become one of my division's top reps by billing (number one by a fair margin some months) and I was probably in the top five by paycheck size, about $10,000 per year less than at least one other rep who had a more advantageous bonus structure. Who cares. More importantly, specific dollar amounts *do not matter*. My plan has no tie to such specifics.

It's all about getting to a lifestyle that is pleasing to *you*, with most or all of the "fat" cut out of it, then setting up a situation in which you're able to fund that same lifestyle with possible room for future expansion of the pleasure. This is not about the Jones family next door; it's about you. In fact, forgetting about what other people have and what they're doing is central to success. So we don't need to talk about income specifics, or exact totals of nest eggs needed, or anything of the sort. Each person's situation and financial requirements are different. The devil is in the details, so we will concentrate on the generalities. You'll come to see that percentages are more useful than specific dollar amounts. It's how this works!

I spent my last several working years living on 30% of my income. Let that sink in for a minute. I didn't make that much, and I lived on 30% of my income. For years. What the hell?! *No way*, you're thinking. *I should just stop reading right now. This guy is full of it.* Well guess what. I am not full of it. I put 70% of my income toward my future, while living a perfectly fantastic present including vacations in San Diego, Palm Springs, Florida (a few times), Spain, Costa Rica (twice), and Mexico (twice). I also bought wedding rings and paid for a wedding, took care of a $2300 tree removal emergency and a surprise $1500 medical bill, replaced a dead washing machine and three kitchen appliances, donated to my favorite charities, and drank lots of expensive micro-brewery beer. I'm drinking one right now, as a matter of fact. I just happen to be drinking it at home where it's one third the price I'd pay at the local pub (a savings of 67% not including tip, you know).

Just as my efforts were kicking into high gear, I came across a study indicating that saving 70% of current income could be expected to result in maintainable and safe early retirement in seven years assuming proper investment of the savings and historically-average market returns. I examined the research and studied the numbers, and determined that the information was accurate. Saving more (yeah right) would result in crossing the line earlier, and saving less would get me there a bit later. 70% seemed like a lot, but I made that my goal. Later, when I realized I was on track, I was kind of shocked. Because it didn't even hurt!

A big reason I was able to make quick, consistent progress was my ability to avoid a trap that catches most of us. We don't even notice it happening until we're already in the trap and stuck in a pattern of *lifestyle creep* or *lifestyle inflation*. It's a pretty simple concept, and an important one. Avoiding this trap is crucial for anyone who wants to get ahead. The point here is one of my guiding principles, major enough to warrant its own paragraph.

If your life is already satisfactory and/or satisfying and your income increases (or you get a one-time influx of cash like an inheritance), direct the new money into savings rather than inflating a lifestyle that doesn't need to be improved just because it's possible. Avoid lifestyle creep.

More money will bring more choices. If you come into some extra money, it's up to you to decide if you want to stick with the old car that's getting you around town with no issues, or if you want something newer and shinier because "it'll feel good." Keep the big picture in mind at all times. You were already happy. Will you be happier in the long run if you blow a bunch of money on a new car, or if you save that money and get yourself to financial independence earlier? If getting out of the rat race sooner is important, I say stick with the perfectly acceptable status quo and quietly put the money toward the end-goal. How much will the more-expensive vacation enhance your life? How much will the larger house (which can be filled with more crap you don't really need) in the higher-end neighborhood (with higher property taxes) improve your daily existence? We have choices when we come into extra "disposable income." We can make these choices without regard to what most others are doing. Sometimes the best option is to stick with the life we were already enjoying, and not "dispose" of the extra income at all. When my income increased a bit, I didn't change anything other than the pace of my saving and investing. Sticking with the same house and the same car and the same old clothes made a difference of, literally, years.

Because my job got completely out of hand (as we've discussed) and my financial progress was ahead of schedule, I ended up jumping a little early. It helps more than a little that I can get spousal health insurance via Dave's job (thanks to the marriage equality ruling in 2015) until later when our combined income is lower and I can shop the ACA insurance marketplace with the possibility of finding a better deal. Or perhaps my dream of better health insurance options in the U.S. will come true in the near future. Of course if we end up in any other civilized country, where health care isn't a profit machine for a small number of rich people, this point will be moot...but I digress. (Sorry. Can you tell I have a bee in my pants over our country's health care system?)

Suffice to say, I got there. The investing part is crucial, but if you don't save anything you don't have anything to invest. So how in the world did I manage to live on so little without even suffering? Let's look into it.

Redefining a Life Well-Lived (or, Budget Schmudget)

Conventional wisdom involves "paying yourself first" and setting up a budget, putting aside a set amount of money out of each paycheck to go into savings and then attempting to spend predetermined amounts on everyday expenses until the next paycheck arrives. I say hogwash. Actually, I say it in all caps. HOGWASH. I think this advice is absolutely terrible. Why in the world would a person with free will and freedom of spending choice want to put limits on how much might be saved? To me, this whole budgeting concept comes across as ridiculous. It may work for some, but seriously...if you can't control yourself and your spending impulses, how can you expect to get ahead? I say this: when it comes to saving money, the sky is the limit. The amount you want to save is equal to the entire amount you don't spend. Period. I think budgets for the individual are a poor idea. Wait; that's not strong enough. I think budgets for the individual (or couple, or family) are freaking stupid. There's a sentence up there that is important enough that I should say it again, give it its own paragraph, and call it one of my guiding principles.

The amount you want to save is equal to the entire amount you don't spend.

There is a difference between *creating a budget* and *studying what is being spent every month on each category of expenses.* The latter is something I do highly (very highly) recommend, especially at the outset of a big, life-changing strategy shift like, say, getting financially smart in order to beat The Man and retire early. It doesn't have to be complicated or difficult; it can be done in five minutes. Just sit down with an open spreadsheet or a piece of paper, and estimate what's being spent on everything. Cross-referencing with actual banking records is the way to go, because there may be some surprises. The first time I looked at my spending habits, I was shocked to see how much of my money was going toward groceries and bars/restaurants. Obviously, the categories in which we spend the most are the ones where we have the opportunity to save the most. So knowing where all the money is going every month is important. But, in my strong opinion, deciding in advance how much to spend in each category going forward is not necessary or even a good idea. It's just too easy at the end of the month to say, "Oh look, I have $20 left to spend on Miscellaneous Leisure Activities so I should go out tonight!"

I never wanted to determine in advance how much I was going to put aside for the future. It made more sense to me to do things in reverse. I chose and choose to spend as little as necessary to provide a pleasing life, and save the rest. Doesn't this make more sense? It's so easy! All one needs is a shift in mindset, a "paradigm shift" if you will, that guides the flow of all financial resources and ensures (or at least encourages) their movement to the destination that results in optimum happiness.

This brings us to another of my guiding principles. This is of extreme importance, and I recommend that you read it several times before going any further. This ultra-important concept gets its own paragraph. Before I spend even one dollar, ever, I stop and automatically ask myself this question:

Will the product or experience I'm about to purchase enhance my life more than achieving financial independence sooner? Do I choose to work longer for this expense?

If the answer is "yes," I gladly spend. If the answer is "no," I put that cash (or my debit card, or my cash-back credit card I'll pay off before I'm charged interest) back in my pocket. Because the goal is *the best possible life*, not something as small as "saving money" or "buying something" or the vague "getting ahead" or the dreaded and dangerous "ooh I want that product or experience and I deserve it." The goal is to make the best possible use of every single dollar.

At first, this may seem kind of irritating. *How can a person live this way?* I was fortunate, because I got most of the way there before I even realized I was doing it. It became automatic. Then it even became fun. It's still fun. "Do I want to color my facial hair? Hm. Nah, I'll save that five bucks and invest it, and ten years from now I'll have turned it into fifteen bucks and I can buy lunch during retirement." I know that five dollars sounds like a pretty small deal, but we're not talking about the specific amount. We're talking about the mindset. And once this new mindset is in place and fully operational and dependable, it starts kicking in across-the-board. Small amounts make a difference, larger amounts make a larger difference, and *all* amounts make all the difference.

That said, let me divulge that I don't make optimal use of every single dollar. That's not my style. I knew from the start that I wanted a plan that gave me some flexibility, because if I got too strict with myself I'd never stick with the plan. A "slip" every now and then is built into the system, and can make life more enjoyable overall. For me, this is essential. If there's a small earthquake every now and then, maybe the San Andreas Fault won't slip all at once and send Los Angeles into the ocean. I feel like my spending works the same way. I like going out to dinner every now and then, and I don't worry too much about the cost. If I did it every night, my food expenses would skyrocket and I'd have to work until I'm dead. I'm sure I had to work a few extra months because of those times I didn't make my margaritas at home. Whatever. That's what we call balance. (But once I realized that my homemade margaritas are better, and don't contain corn syrup or food color, and cost about fifty cents to make…yeah, I ended up liking them a lot more than the nasty ones at the Mexican restaurant down the street.)

At first, it may seem like this "mindset" thing can't possibly make much of a difference. *So I skip a dinner out every once in a while*, you're thinking. *How is fifty bucks going to change my life?* Let's take a look at this question, and turn it into actual dollar amounts I'll explain in more detail in the investing section, later. For the sake of simplicity, we'll look at a 20-year period and see what can happen to our financial situation in that time frame once we make some lifestyle changes (some easy, some a little more difficult) and put the savings to work. I'm pulling the 20-year concept from thin air, just so we have something on which to base the numbers. Remember, we're more interested in general concepts than specifics, and this will give you an idea of how much of a difference each eliminated unnecessary expense can make.

I'll list ten randomly-selected changes we made at our house, to illustrate the point. Some (like refinancing a loan or updating an insurance policy) are one-time changes that require a bit of leg work and/or angst, then provide savings every month going forward. Others (like changing buying habits) are more of an ongoing project but offer similar long-term benefits. In all cases, the payoff is higher than one might expect. It's likely that some of these may apply to your specific situation, and others may not.

The "BMD" noted under each item is what I call the "Beat-the-Man Difference." This amount is what I consider the total, actual reward we receive for each reduction in monthly expenditures. It's the sum of how much we'll no longer need (because we'll be spending less), and how much more we'll now end up having (because we'll be investing our savings). It will be explained in more detail after we look at the examples, listed in order from low-dollar to high-dollar. Some dollar amounts are estimated. Let's take a look!

Reduced/Eliminated Ongoing Expenses and Associated BMD after 20 Years

Replaced Most Light Bulbs with Compact Fluorescents and Adjusted Thermostat
Monthly savings (less bulb-replacing, lower electric bills): $10
Invested monthly over 20 years, transforms into: $5,929
Reduction in cash needed for the next 20 years: $2,400
Total BMD: $8,329

Stopped Buying Bakery/Grocery Bread, Switched to Homemade
Monthly savings: $15
Invested monthly over 20 years, transforms into: $8,894
Reduction in cash needed for the next 20 years: $3,600
Total BMD: $12,494

Cancelled Gym Membership in Favor of Working Out at Home
Monthly savings: $20
Invested monthly over 20 years, transforms into: $11,859
Reduction in cash needed for the next 20 years: $4,800
Total BMD: $16,659

Cut Car Insurance on Old Vehicle to Liability-Only
Monthly savings: $33
Invested monthly over 20 years, transforms into: $19,567
Reduction in cash needed for the next 20 years: $7,920
Total BMD: $27,487

Concentrated on Grocery Bargain Stock-Ups (Costco, Aldi, etc.)
Monthly savings: $40
Invested monthly over 20 years, transforms into: $23,718
Reduction in cash needed for the next 20 years: $9,600
Total BMD: $33,318

Reduced Restaurant Meals by 1-2 per Month
Monthly savings: $50
Invested monthly over 20 years, transforms into: $29,647
Reduction in cash needed for the next 20 years: $12,000
Total BMD: $41,647

Dropped Life Insurance Once Nest Egg Could Cover Lost Income
Monthly savings: $80
Invested monthly over 20 years, transforms into: $47,436
Reduction in cash needed for the next 20 years: $19,200
Total BMD: $66,636

Replaced Bar Happy Hours with Beers on Back Deck at Home
Monthly savings: $100
Invested monthly over 20 years, transforms into: $59,295
Reduction in cash needed for the next 20 years: $24,000
Total BMD: $83,295

Dropped Cable TV for Digital Broadcast Antenna, Amazon Prime, Sling TV App
Monthly savings: $140
Invested monthly over 20 years, transforms into: $83,013
Reduction in cash needed for the next 20 years: $33,600
Total BMD: $116,613

Refinanced Mortgage under HARP Program
Monthly savings: $200
Invested monthly over 20 years, transforms into: $118,589
Reduction in cash needed for the next 20 years: $48,000*
Total BMD: $166,589

Does not include big savings on actual loan due to lower interest rate.

So this BMD, the "Beat-the-Man Difference," is a rather important concept, and it's somewhat...obtuse. It takes a while for this idea to sink into the brain, but I recommend spending the time to internalize it because it accurately reflects the true difference each spending/lifestyle change makes in the long run, and encourages thoughtful life improvements that bring happiness. It also illustrates the fact that making adjustments that will be ongoing can make a dramatic difference in how much money one will eventually *need* in order to retire, and also how much money one will eventually *have* to make it possible earlier. Basically, we're creating a situation in which we end up needing less money than we once thought we would, *and* we're ending up with more money in our possession. Obviously this is pretty great.

It's kind of like trying to lose weight. If you diet, you lose weight. If you exercise, you lose weight. If you diet and exercise concurrently, you're attacking the situation from both sides and making an exponentially more dramatic difference. By attacking your financial situation from both sides, you're increasing the amount of money you have, *and* you're reducing the amount of money you're going to need. Extra credit!

At our house, just the ten examples of life adjustment noted above made a long-term difference of over half a million dollars! The reduction in how much money we'll need to fund our lives over the next twenty years *plus* the extra money we can expect to have on hand as a result of investing the savings? It's a whopping $573,067. As you can see, reducing the amount that will eventually be needed is a big part of the plan, and where it all begins.

I've read countless articles documenting why the average American will need crazy sums of money to fund retirement. These articles are often written by "investment professionals" who make a living handling people's life savings for a percentage, as long as the money stays in an account that can be managed. Or they appear in publications that cater to the self-diagnosed "affluent" who exist in circles where conspicuous consumption is and will always be a way of life. News flash! Those of us who are interested in living sensibly and are willing to learn how to manage our own investments do not need, oh, $2.4 million or whatever the trendy number is this month.

Later, we'll discuss some investing specifics and I'll explain how something as simple as cutting the cable TV cord can end up putting more than $80,000 in your pocket twenty years later if you invest your savings monthly. If this seems outlandish or mystifying right now, don't worry. We'll get there. Right now, just go with me. As a sneak preview, and for the benefit of those who may be at least somewhat familiar with the markets, I'll mention that I've assumed an historically-conservative 8% after-tax total return annually on our investments (including dividends) to come up with the "invested monthly over 20 years" results in the examples above. There is absolutely no way to know precisely how much the stock market will go up or down at any time, of course. Honestly, I expect returns that far exceed 8% over the long haul, on average. But I'd rather end up with too much money than too little, so I went with what is, historically, on the low end of what is reasonably likely.

One more important caveat is that the big BMD totals above assume that we're not taking any of this money *out* of investments to cover living expenses for twenty years. The "reduction in cash needed for the next 20 years" figures will be solid (and are actually conservative, with inflation likely to increase the price of everything as time passes). But once we leave the workforce and begin to strategically pull money out of our investments to cover the cost of life, obviously our returns will be affected. There are ways to minimize this effect, and we'll discuss them later.

While we're still on the general topic of saving, where we've seen that adjustments to ongoing expenses can make the biggest long-term difference, let's also discuss one-time expenses and "every once in a while" expenses. Things pop up in life. Once you've begun to develop a new attitude about pulling each dollar out of your wallet, you'll probably begin to look at life's random emergencies and unplanned expenses from a different perspective (a more negative one!). Try not to sweat it. You'll have an emergency fund in place (this is a very important topic we'll cover shortly), and this is where you'll go for funds to cover non-recurring expenses. I also include "special big-ticket self-treat"-type outlays in this general category.

When dealing with a non-recurring expense, I turn to another guiding principle. This one is pretty obvious, and really simple. The only difficult part? Remembering to actually follow it, when possible, *every time* a non-recurring expense occurs. These guiding principles get their own paragraph, of course. Here it is.

When you want or need to spend money on an item or experience, take time to consider all options to satisfy that want or need. Then select the option that offers the most value.

This does *not* mean I always go with the cheapest option. We wouldn't buy a $50 car, right? It would be likely to break down the very day we bought it, and $50 would have been wasted. But I wouldn't want the brand new luxury SUV for $50,000 either. That's more vehicle than I would want or need. I'd want to take a look at assorted pre-owned options in a more sensible price range, come up with a set of possible vehicles I could buy with cash that would be likely to satisfy me for many years, and choose the one that was the best value for the money.

Another example of this concept is the way I like to plan vacations. Last year I was looking at a once-in-a-lifetime expense: a honeymoon. This is kind of a biggie, obviously. I have this dream of taking a trip to the Greek islands. As our stash of savings grew, I was more and more tempted to bring this dream to fruition when it was time to plan a honeymoon (what a great excuse, right?). But when I checked on the details, not knowing special tricks to cut the cost (there are always special tricks) and not having the time to find them at the height of my work-related stress period, it looked like the cost of such a dream trip was going to be upwards of $4000 per person to do it right. This was entirely unacceptable. So I started looking at other destinations that might cost a lot less but still offer beautiful scenery with striking ocean views and some sort of interesting, unfamiliar culture. I asked myself what other options might cover my "want." I landed on Puerto Vallarta, Mexico. We got dirt-cheap flights and after days of searching I found a character-filled boutique hotel on a mountain river several blocks from the ocean in an authentic Mexican neighborhood. The cost of the hotel, which had a rooftop pool overlooking the mountains and city, and featured artsy and romantic rooms furnished with pieces from old films, was $62 per night off-season. Our room had a big balcony overlooking the river. It was fantastic. We loved our week so much that we went back the following spring, stayed in the condo with the roosters across the street, and researched local rentals for possible retirement relocation. I could have paid five times as much, noticeably affecting my early retirement plan. Instead, I found a wholly satisfying alternative and sacrificed nothing. I still want to see the Greek islands, of course, but I need to find some cost-saving tricks first. Otherwise a cheaper trip will continue to be a better life-enhancing value.

Sometimes a non-recurring expense can't be comparison-shopped. If, say, you get hit in the head with a huge iron pipe and have to go to the emergency room (this happened to me...let's not dwell on such unpleasant trauma), there may be no way to cut corners. But often, a little work can result in great savings. I'll list some random examples of success stories here at our house. Maybe some of these will stick with you and inspire future victories. We'll start with some small ones, and look at them in ascending order by price point.

Non-Recurring Expenses Knocked Down to a Minimum

Dave's Workplace Pot-Luck Lunches
Boy oh boy. Once you get serious about saving for early retirement, is there anything more irritating than being pressured to use the money you made at work to pay for food you have to prepare or purchase during your precious free time you've earned so you can take a pot luck dish to...work? I've been fortunate to escape these, but poor Dave used to get suckered into them all the time. These days, he often makes some polite excuse and "can't take part in this one."
Savings: $10-15 per occurrence

Guitar Strings
I mentioned while socializing with friends that I was out of guitar strings. A friend who works at Guitar Center happened to have a huge stash of them from an expired promotion (he grabbed them for $1 per set), and offered a bunch to me for free. They weren't my normal brand, but I tried them and liked them. I told him I'd buy him a beer some time. (This is kind of what is called the "shared economy." It's a big trend, actually...kind of like a private version of socialism, maybe. There are online communities coordinating such swaps, though usually not for beer. In my peer group, beer is part of the shared economy.)
Savings: $20

Aw Crap, the Washing Machine Broke
Our three-year-old modern washer stopped agitating, causing much agitation. "Doesn't that thing know I'm trying to retire?!" A home fix-it effort failed, then a pro repair guy informed us that the problem was most likely going to involve a $350 motherboard replacement. We found a great pre-owned washing machine on Craig's List for $100. Now our clothes are actually cleaner, and we do not have a motherboard in our washer.
Savings: $400

A New Sofa

I kind of have a mental block concerning pre-owned furniture (are there scary bugs in it?), so when our super-nasty couch needed to go, we scoured online sites for deals and info, then hit about ten furniture stores in one afternoon and sat on about four million sofas. We came up with a list of all acceptable options, then found the one that looked like the best value on that very store's web site for less during a holiday weekend sale. We called the store for a price match and got what we wanted for the lowest possible price.

Savings: $500

Clothes for the Work Convention

Working in a home office for many years has allowed me to stick with a pretty small wardrobe. An annual work convention involved a fair number of photos, and interaction with a lot of the same people year after year. Wearing the exact same collared shirts every convention could eventually be noticed, so I'd freshen the convention look with a trip to the Goodwill for cheap shirts someone else got tired of wearing. Why pay five times as much for a shirt, when there are hundreds of them at the thrift store and nobody will ever know the difference? (And, less waste for the planet. Recycling!) People aren't as likely to notice pants or fit them into the pictures, so I didn't worry so much about that part. I actually wore the same pair of dress pants to the Saturday night dressy dinner ten years in a row and I don't think anyone ever noticed.

Savings: $800-plus over the years

The Cost of Publishing This Book

I could pay a fair amount of money to order a stack of physical versions of this book once it's finished (it will be self-published). But I know from my experience releasing CDs on my own label that it's somewhat likely I'll end up with boxes and boxes of physical product taking up space in my house while most sales will be digital, so at the outset I'm going e-book only. Also, I could forego the angst of learning how to convert my file to e-book format and enlist the services of helpful individuals who'd like to help in return for a percentage of all future sales, forever. In case people actually end up buying this, I don't like that idea. I like passive income when it's mine, not when I'm providing it to someone else!

Savings: $700-plus, and more pennies for each book download forever

Oh No! The HVAC Crap-Out!

We have a 25-year-old HVAC unit, so it's only a matter of time until we're hit with a big expense. The thing stopped working a couple of years back and we thought it was The End (ouch). Did you know that these days you can search YouTube and find out how to fix just about anything? People love to fix stuff, then post helpful how-to videos. We found one of a guy fixing an old split unit just like ours, and Dave took his laptop to the basement, let the video play next to the dead blower, and followed the guy's recommendations. After a couple of hours of scraping, vacuuming, cleaning, and cussing...success! It's still working. For now, we've saved a bundle. And leaving that pile of money in investments has simultaneously made us a bit of an extra bundle as well.

Savings: $4000-5000

Dan's Latest CD

I'm a Nashville-based singer/songwriter with six CDs to my credit and a seventh almost finished. (Side note: the new one will include a song called "Me Against the Man" because...why not. It was a song before it was a book!) Partly to save money and mostly because I enjoy having complete creative control, I play all the instruments and sing all or almost all of the vocal parts myself. I write all of the songs, with an occasional cowriter if the mood strikes. I handle the production and the engineering, and record in a home studio. I design the artwork. I do pay for mastering (after lots of comparison shopping) and duplication of a small run of physical product. Thousands of artists here and elsewhere spend many thousands of dollars to make a record. Mine cost maybe a couple hundred bucks all-in. I can't say for sure that I'll never

commission the help of professionals I'll need to pay well, but so far I've managed to create a lot of pretty good music without spending much money. This way, when I sell a copy I'm not just recouping expenses.
Savings: $5000-plus per CD

Wedding Bells
I wouldn't have thought it possible even a few years ago, but we were able to get married last year. So many young couples spend truckloads of money on expensive weddings. In my opinion, this is very sad. That money, spent on a few hours of impressiveness, could be the foundation of a better life. I know it's a once-in-a-lifetime event (assuming you're marrying the right person). Of course it should be really special. But if by "special" you mean hundreds of guests gathered in a rented hall eating and drinking expensive dinners and beverages served by a staff of waiters and waitresses with some DJ cranking out "Celebration," "YMCA," and "Mony Mony"...no thanks. We're fortunate to have a group of friends who are incredibly creative, industrious, and open-minded. They're also good cooks. We had a pot-luck event at a friend's house, beautifully decorated for the occasion. We were surrounded by a small group of nineteen dear human beings, and it was magical and perfect. The net cost was a few hundred bucks at most. As a bonus, we bought our wedding rings in Mexico during the honeymoon we took *before* the wedding. We had a blast exploring shops and street vendor stands, found exactly what we wanted, and spent a grand total of 850 pesos (a little more than $50 U.S.) for both rings. Thinking outside the box can bring great rewards!
Savings: $10,000 and up, up, up to the ridiculous stratosphere (wedding and rings)

Look at all that saving! I do find it increasingly fun to not waste money, and I could talk about it ad nauseam (my friends will testify to the fact that I sometimes do). I'll include more exhaustive lists of money-saving ideas at the end of the book. But we have other matters to discuss right now, like what to do with all that saved money.   Before we leave this section that's specifically about saving, I'd like to point out something important.   None of the specific ongoing cost-cuts or non-recurring expenses tackled efficiently and discussed above involved or involve any noticeable reduction in quality of life.   Some of our moves have involved periods of adjustment, doing without fun toys that all the cool kids seem to be enjoying, remaining less fashionable than the Hiltons and living in a smaller house than the Joneses, etc.   But we have other priorities, and we enjoy our lives.   And we enjoy the balances on our credit cards, because they are zero.   This last sentence leads us directly to our next sub-topic.

Debt = Poison

Now that we've started to save a bunch of cash, we're almost ready to figure out what to do with it so we can make it start turning itself into more cash.   But first, we have to check to see if we have a nasty, nasty, nasty problem to eliminate before we can even think about investing.   That gigantic problem we don't want in our lives is debt.

Not all debt is bad.   Early in life, it can be advantageous to carry a little debt and then pay it off quickly and efficiently to increase a credit score that will come in handy.   Debt carried for no more than a few weeks on the right credit card that gets paid off before any interest accrues can result in nice perks like cash back or airline miles.   Later in life, it can be smart for even, say, a guy who is retiring early and will be living primarily on savings and passive investment income to continue holding a low-interest-rate mortgage when he could just write a check and pay off the house. Why, you ask? Because that guy knows that he can earn more on that money if it's invested than he will be paying in interest on his mortgage loan.   Here's my general advice, and we'll call it another guiding principle.

Any debt costing more than 5% should be considered a disaster and an emergency. Expensive debt must be attacked and destroyed.

Anyone of modest means intending to be serious about getting ahead financially must address issues involving expensive debt before expecting to make real progress. Saving money and holding it in a low-interest savings or checking account, or opening a certificate of deposit and making 1%, or buying government bonds and making 1.5%, or investing well and making 10% or 12%...none of this makes a lick of sense for a person holding credit card debt costing 15% or 18% or more. We want to make money to fund our own lives, not give our hard-earned dollars to some banking conglomerate CEO. If you have credit card debt, make it your top priority to get rid of it, smash it, destroy it, kill it! My rather stern advice to anyone carrying credit card balances is to consider the situation the disaster that it is. Don't go to the movies, don't go out to dinner, don't buy those concert tickets, don't go to the game, don't buy a shirt, don't buy a coffee at Starbucks (which is sad anyway, unless you think it's fun to pay four bucks for something you can make at home for a dime). If you have credit card debt and you're truly interested in moving toward financial independence, put every extra penny toward paying off the credit cards. And then, never carry a balance again, ever.

I had credit card debt when I was in my twenties. I wanted stuff, and stores and banks were happy to let me pay them interest so I could have that stuff. I carried some of that debt into my thirties. Then one day I discovered that I had a lot more debt than I thought (most of it wasn't my fault, but that's a very long story for another book). I had $36,000 in credit card debt and couldn't even keep up with the monthly payments. I didn't want to file bankruptcy, so I let myself get suckered into what might have been an even worse situation, rolling the debt into a high-interest-rate home refinance loan. A lot happened from there (again, it all belongs in another book), and eventually I walked away from a house on which I'd paid for seven years with nothing. I stayed above water, but just barely. That house is now worth almost four times what I paid for it initially, and I could have made a bundle. But debt was the roadblock between me and financial success.

From the day I signed the refinance papers and in the twelve-plus years since I signed a quit claim deed and walked away from that house, I've never carried a credit card balance of even one cent. I use a card to get the cash-back bonus, but never, ever carry a balance. If you have credit card debt, get that roadblock off your road now, as quickly as you can. You can do it! Really, you must do it. Credit card debt is evil. Once you're rid of your card balances, keep them at zero. Forever. If it's not a house (bought with at least 20% down) or an education, and if you can't buy it with cash, perhaps you should go save more cash before you consider making the purchase. Did I say perhaps? You should.

You'll note that I said, "If it's not a house or an education." We all need some sort of shelter, and most can't afford to buy a home (early in life, at least) without financing the purchase. I recommend a non-ownership living situation (renting, living with family, etc.) until a 20% down payment is possible and practical. This allows for the elimination of PMI (Private Mortgage Insurance), premiums paid to the lender to insure against default on the loan. It's a needless expense. This falls into the "do as I say and not as I did" category (I didn't even know what PMI was when I bought my first house). If you're at least close to being able to come up with 20%, wait until you're there. Importantly, don't buy a huge house you can't afford. It's called a starter home for a reason. You can move later if you like, and you'll enjoy not being stuck under a gigantic mortgage payment. The fact that we have a very low mortgage payment at our house ($700 per month, including taxes and insurance) is key to my ability to declare financial freedom early. I bought what I could more-than-afford at the time, and we've stayed put not just because we like the neighborhood but because we're able to sock away a big portion of our income by keeping our housing costs low. Choosing an apartment or house is often the most important financial decision in a person's life, so let's call this a guiding principle.

Your rent or mortgage payment will likely be your biggest monthly expense. Choose your housing carefully, and view the decision in the context of the rest of your life.

A comfortable and pleasing living environment is of the utmost importance. And if a little extra is going to be spent, real estate is not a bad place to spend it. But think back to the set of recurring expenses I shared earlier, and remember that every bit of extra money going to the mortgage company (or a landlord) and utility companies (more space means higher bills) is money that won't go toward financial independence. We could have moved to a house costing more than twice as much years ago, but I'm retiring early instead. For me, this is a huge win.

For most, I think that owning a home (rather than renting) is an excellent idea. There are tax advantages, and historically the investment is likely to at least keep pace with inflation. A portion of each monthly payment goes into equity rather than into someone else's pocket, and that's quite nice. I happen to have made a wise choice when I bought my house years ago, landing in an increasingly-popular neighborhood in what has since become an "it" city with rapidly rising property values. While we're likely to face rising property taxes in the near future, we have massive equity (the house is presently worth about three times what we still owe) and the situation gave me some of the comfort I needed to begin considering declaring myself financially independent. Of course we could experience another disruption in the housing market in the future, so I tend to look at our equity situation as a bonus rather than a given.

Regarding education and student loans...I was fortunate to not be saddled with debt when I graduated college back in the day. My parents took care of my room and board, and I landed a music scholarship and an academic scholarship to cover all of my tuition. I know that many or most aren't so fortunate. I've picked up virtually no expertise in this area, because it doesn't apply to me. I know that student loans cannot be discharged via bankruptcy, and that the interest rates tend to be high (sadly), and that many need years to pay off gigantic balances. As far as I can tell, there are no magic methods to take care of student loans. I've heard tale of people finding ways to move balances and combine debts and perhaps lower interest rates a bit and perhaps get rid of the debt sooner. But I'm not well-informed on this topic. Remember how I started learning about getting smarter about finances in the first place? I just randomly googled questions and ended up launching an investigation that led to a lot of answers. If I had student loans, I'd probably try the same thing. There are a lot of people with student loan debt in this country, and many are hanging out in online communities sharing success stories. If you have this type of debt, I recommend finding these groups to learn from the experience of others who have come before you.

Should you have children who need money for college now and/or later, I'm afraid I won't be able to share much information of use to you either. I know there are tax-advantaged saving plans that come highly recommended, but this has never applied to me so I've glossed over the whole situation. Again, check out the success stories of others online. Google is your friend. These are huge dollar amounts, so time spent researching how to optimize is time well spent.

Now, how about some quick car talk. We've spent a little time discussing credit card debt and the importance of getting rid of it. By the same token (and this may come as a bit of a surprise to some), anyone paying on a vehicle loan with *any* interest rate should consider this an emergency as well. A vehicle is a depreciating asset. Even a cheap loan for a vehicle is a bad deal for the borrower, because a vehicle depreciates so steadily and dramatically (costing the indebted owner invisible lost money over time). *But everyone needs a car*, you're thinking. First, this may not even be true. Many, many acquaintances of mine in online communities have given up their cars in favor of assorted options as varied as public transportation, bicycles (which are all the rage in some frugal circles), their legs, Lyft and Uber, shared vehicles, and combinations of these and other alternatives. Even automakers are admitting that fewer individuals will own their own cars in the future, as existing options and new technologies change the way we transport ourselves. At this time, having a car for each driver in the household remains an American convenience I've chosen to retain. But at this stage of life, I wouldn't even consider financing a new one, and I'm fairly certain I won't even replace the one I have now if it suffers a major mechanical problem.

We still maintain two vehicles at our house, but will likely go down to just one the next time we face any sort of serious repair bills. I bought my 2001 vehicle with cash eleven years ago, and Dave paid off his 1999 truck many years ago. We don't look very impressive to strangers at intersections, but think back to the recurring expenses information earlier in this book and imagine how much further ahead we are now as a result of not saddling ourselves with car payments for so many years. Considering the cost of a vehicle itself, plus maintenance, plus insurance, plus licensing and registration, plus gas...sheesh, driving is a big expense. And don't forget about depreciation. I dream of life without a car, and I won't be at all surprised if I end up figuring out how to live that way.

Cutting to the chase...should you reach a point at which you feel you must make a vehicle purchase, remember that you're filling a need and buying function, not a shiny toy to impress yourself, your friends, the Joneses, and strangers at intersections. If the goal is financial independence, a vehicle purchase will delay success. Buy what you can afford to buy with cash. They tell me Craig's List is a great place to shop for cars and cut out the dealer and his mark-up. They tell me it's also a great place to sell them. I'll probably start there if I decide to sell mine, and I'm sure we'll take a look if we decide to buy one. And if you've read these last few paragraphs and determined that you may presently own a vehicle that's overly luxurious or expensive, don't be afraid to get rid of that sucker on Craig's List yourself and replace it with something more sensible (or nothing!). And oh my gosh...do NOT lease a vehicle. You want to work toward *eliminating* one of your largest monthly expenses, not ensure that you'll be throwing away money every month forever. No leasing of a car, please.

Okay, now that we've spent some time dealing with debt and getting it out of our way (did I mention that it's evil?), we have one additional topic to cover before we're ready to invest. It's something we can tackle as we begin investing, actually, and it's very simple.

Emergencies Happen: Build an Emergency Fund

An emergency fund is the liquid, quickly-accessible cash you keep nearby in case of, duh, emergencies. Unexpected expenses of varying severity happen. That's how life works. A recent survey conducted by the *Washington Post* indicated that 46% of Americans don't have enough cash on hand to cover a $400 emergency. Another recent poll published by *Forbes* decried the fact that 63% of Americans couldn't cover a $500 mishap. It seems that about half of us are one small surprise away from being in trouble. This is disturbing. Having an emergency fund in place before you really start rolling down the road to financial independence is crucial. This fund is important for several reasons.

> 1. It makes for a better, more relaxing existence. I've lived life one big expense away from being wiped out, and more recently I've lived life not having to balance my checkbook and instead being able to just scan my checking account for suspicious charges, check my emergency fund balance, and

throw everything extra into my investments a few times a month. Guess which way of life is more enjoyable.

2. It allows you to stay out of debt. Remember that if you need money quickly and have to use a credit card, you're going to end up with expensive, nasty debt that adds costs to what you've already had to spend on your emergency. Let's not do that! You can borrow from yourself when a crisis occurs, then pay yourself back at zero percent interest. Please note that this is 100% cheaper.

3. It allows you to maximize the performance of your investments. You know the old adage, "buy low, sell high," right? If all of your cash is tied up in your investments and you suddenly need cash to cover an emergency, you might need to sell something when the market has just suffered a big drop ("sell low" and take a loss) rather than just letting your investments sit until the market recovers. It's even worse if you have to withdraw funds from a tax-deferred account such as a 401k; even if you don't sell when the market is down you'll get hit with taxes and early withdrawal penalties, *and* lose the future earnings on that money. This isn't how we want to do things.

It's guiding principle time!

Don't add unnecessary stress to your life, and don't risk having to spend money to access money that is already yours. Maintain an adequate emergency fund.

It's obvious that an emergency fund is something you'll want to have in place. Once you've begun to reduce expenses and you see some extra cash making its way into your life, and once you've taken care of any debt costing you more than 5%, it's time to enthusiastically fill that emergency fund. It's important enough that if you decided to start putting just a little into this fund while still paying off the last of your credit card debt, I might not even argue. But how much do you need?

Ah, this is a hotly-debated topic on all the early retirement and frugality message boards and online discussion sites, and among supposed "experts." Opinions vary. Some say a year. Some say a couple of months. Entertaining finance guru Suze Orman swears by eight months. Some suggest keeping almost no cash on hand and setting up a home equity line of credit that can be accessed at a low interest rate (and paid off quickly) if there's an emergency. Do you know who is correct? Everybody. And nobody. That's what I say, anyway. I think that the amount an individual should keep in an emergency fund is the amount that *that individual* feels comfortable having set aside in case it's needed. You'll want to have at least enough to cover several months of normal expenses in your emergency fund. Beyond that, in addition to your own instinct, I'll recommend a few other considerations.

How stable is your job, and how long do you think (knowing yourself and your field) it would take you to find a new one if you lost your income? You'll need more than enough to cover that much time in your emergency fund. How is your health, and how is the health of those who depend on you? How old is your car, and how likely is it to break down soon? What other emergencies might hit, and how much would they cost? Might you be taking a vacation soon? (This is one I, personally, sometimes have to remember. I let my emergency fund get a little bloated before planning leisure trips, pay for them with a cash-back credit card, then pay off the card before even departing. Due to workplace stress, vacations have qualified as emergencies here for years!) What amount makes you feel comfortable?

It may presently be a little difficult to imagine (if you're just getting started), but in time you'll come to think of your emergency fund and any separate non-investment account(s) like a checking account, etc., as your "now money" and your investment accounts as your "future money." Once you begin investing in earnest, you'll be buying...monitoring and adjusting on occasion...and holding.

You'll be in this pattern for a long time. The goal (and the reality) will be that your invested money is something you won't touch for years. So spend some time deciding how much you want in your emergency fund, and know that you can always change your mind later and make it larger or smaller.

Personally, I like a healthy emergency fund. Right now, I've let it balloon because I'm about to say goodbye to most of my income and it's appropriate for me to be holding extra cash to cover living expenses. If the market drops, I don't want to be selling any shares. I'll need to be able to wait out even a long-term market correction if necessary. But I've always felt comfortable with an emergency fund that's larger than what most of my early-retirement peers would feel is optimal. I've generally kept mine at a total slightly above a year's worth of normal expenses (which would equal, as you may recall from earlier, about 30% of my income) and I've let it balloon even further as retirement approaches. This isn't what I'd recommend; for most, it's probably way too much when that money could be earning more money for me if I invested it. But it's what has felt comfortable to me. It will be up to you to determine what feels right to *you*.

The other conundrum regarding an emergency fund is…where should it be kept? It probably makes the most sense to put it where it can earn some decent interest, though the price for keeping this money liquid is unimpressive earnings no matter where you stash it. Some use a high-interest online savings account (Ally is a popular bank for this, and other possibilities can be found with a quick online search). Others use credit union checking accounts. Others use a money market fund within an investment account. Conversations on this topic in the online communities get quite involved, and I stay out of them because…well…because I choose to miss out on a couple hundred bucks in interest every year by keeping a sizable portion of my emergency fund in my checking account. There are a lot of boring reasons I made this choice. Mostly it all boils down to this being what I determined would work best for me in a big-picture sense. Some might say I'm being foolish letting that extra interest go to waste, but hey…I'm retiring early, so maybe I kind of know what I'm doing.

I've recently rethought the situation and moved a chunk of my emergency fund into a "high interest" (it's all relative) online savings account at Ally bank. The process was painless and quick (I took care of it online in less than ten minutes), and the money will be easily accessible if I need it. I'm only earning 1% (this rate will rise should inflation take hold going forward), but that's one hundred times as much as I'd earn with a savings account at a traditional brick-and-mortar bank these days. There is no good reason to maintain a savings account or money market account at a traditional bank paying virtually no interest when online options keep an emergency fund just as accessible and safe. I recommend checking out current rates at **www.bankrate.com** to see which institutions are presently offering the best situation. It's an easy thing to do.

Speaking of doing things, are you ready for your head to *really* start spinning? Let's talk about investing! Aw yeah!

THE SOLUTION, PART 2: INVESTING

Okay, here we go.   It's time to dive into the intimidating, complicated, boring, impossibly and absolutely awful topic of investing! Yes! That's how I thought I'd feel about it, too. Imagine my horror when I realized that I had come up with a plan that could get me out of the wrong life and into the right one, but I would have to learn about freaking *investing*. Yikes! Seriously?

Then I started reading. And watching. And talking to smart people. And reading more. And watching more. And talking to more smart people. And realizing that it was actually kind of interesting, and not so intimidating, and quite likely to be something I could not just understand...but something I could learn to do well. I determined early in my process that if I really wanted to transform my life and do it relatively quickly, I would have to somehow convince myself that investing was my new voluntary, enjoyable obsession. Miraculously, I succeeded. I still spend at least an hour every day and/or evening (usually many hours) checking the markets, studying what my funds and individual stocks are doing, reading articles, learning and learning and learning. I usually wake up an hour early so I can get started before I even get out of bed. I can't believe it, but I really like it! Fortunately for you, it won't be necessary for *you* to develop an obsession. I can share the basics with you, and if you want to get obsessed it'll be your own business.

Speaking of you, I'm going to say something very important for your benefit right now. It's for my benefit too, I think.

Do your own research, and a lot of it, before making any financial moves. This book is one person's set of opinions, and that person

does not want to be considered a single, all-knowing source for any investing information or advice offered. Make this book one of many sources you consider before investing. And give your personal wants and needs (present and future) and your ability (or lack thereof) to tolerate temporary losses lots and lots of weight.

I'll share plenty of generic information, and include plenty of comments regarding specific strategies that have worked (and not worked) for me in particular. There certainly isn't one right way to do this, and my way certainly isn't the greatest strategy ever created or even the best strategy for all people. But it has worked and is working, so we'll take a look at what I'm doing.

If you're ex-military and have certain investment options I don't have (because I'm not ex-military), I don't understand them so I won't cover them. If you're a teacher or government employee and have another set of investment options I don't have (because I'm not a teacher or government employee), ditto. The self-employed also have options I've not researched because my self-employment side-income is a very small part of my financial picture. I was already middle-aged when I really dove into this, and I wanted to progress quickly so I could, uh, save my own life. I concentrated on learning just what I thought would get me where I, in particular, needed to go. There's plenty I don't yet know, but what I do know seems to have been the right stuff. I hope you'll enjoy checking out what I have to say keeping in mind that these are investment basics mixed with a little complicated nuance here and there to create a plan appropriate for those with fairly high risk tolerance looking to get financially healthier with a bit of a casual attitude.

And here's one last caveat, which I'm adding (and putting in italics to make it stand out a bit) a while after this book was originally completed. I came up with my own successful combination of investing strategies and the plan to cover my financial needs for the rest of my days under the assumption that our planet and its financial structures would not encounter anything completely unlike any and all events in generations of history going back to the nineteenth century. It's important for me to state, right here, that the surprise results of the November 2016 election in the U.S. may qualify as this type of event. I strongly suspect that markets will be in for a period of rather dramatic adjustment, and caution will be a very good idea. If you're reading this after hearing about a major market crash, know that your timing is probably great and you'll have the opportunity to get in at the bottom and increase your financial well-being dramatically during the recovery. If not, consider concentrating on your saving for the time being, and keep your eyes and ears open for major domestic and international events that could soon affect economies here and abroad. The markets always go up eventually, but we are probably heading into some crazy times.

Why Invest in the Stock Market?

Now there's a good question, and an important one to ask! There are other options for turning savings into more savings, after all. Starting a business and actually becoming The Man (or The Woman) is a great way to get ahead, if the business idea is viable and the individual has the appropriate *let's do this* personality and proper resources. But starting a business can be risky. One of my closest friends gave this strategy a shot, with a great concept and adequate time and money at the ready. We all thought she was destined for greatness, but profits never materialized and she's closing up shop as I type this sentence. Real estate is another common road. I have several friends who have done well putting their cash into real estate, flipping houses for a profit and/or holding multiple properties and living on rental income resulting from long-term arrangements or short-term agreements forged on airbnb.com and vrbo.com. One acquaintance got started by filling her house with bunk beds and renting to airline pilots and assorted travelling professionals in need of short-term sleeping space, eventually acquiring multiple properties and converting to lower-impact long-term rental income. She now lives on a sailboat with her husband and cat, with monthly income funding adventurous, off-the-grid joy while she pays her mom to manage her properties.

I considered some of these other options, but ultimately decided that I liked my life the way it was except for the "job" part, and would rather just let my saved money do the working so I could eventually have time to enjoy more of what I was already enjoying. I wanted to get rid of something that was taking the majority of my time, and not replace it with something else that would take the same amount of time (or more). I wanted passive income and eventual financial security. Thus, investing.

But the stock market is so risky! Is that what you're thinking? I thought that, at first, before I started learning. History is a great text book, and we have generations of history at our fingertips. If you're looking to get rich quickly by investing in just a few companies hoping for a quick score, or by throwing a bunch of money into the market and planning to make a bundle and pull the money back out in a year or two...yes, that's risky. And that's not smart. The longer your time horizon is and the more strategically diversified your investment portfolio becomes, the more safety you afford yourself and your nest egg.

Investing in the stock market becomes infinitely safer when viewed as part of a long-term strategy designed to result in big-picture life enjoyment.

Imagine, if you will, a rectangle. Place your index finger at the lower left corner of the rectangle, then drag it gradually up and to the right, all the way to the top right corner. This is the direction in which the value of stocks has moved over generations. It goes up, it goes down, then it goes up a little more than it went down, then it drops again, then it goes up a little further. We can't know with certainty what the market will do in the short term, but in the long term it has always risen. Always.

Before there were computers, or airplanes, or cars, or relatives of ours who have been born and lived and died...there was the stock market. Our planet has seen industries transformed by technological revolutions, borders redrawn in regional conflicts and world wars, masses traumatized by the Great Depression and the Great Recession. Through all of this history, the stock market has never seen a single twenty-year period in which the market, as an aggregate, was down. Think about this! Even if you had put all of your money into the stock market the day before the great crash in 1929 and lost almost everything the next day, you would only have lost all that money *on paper*. Had you just let it sit, riding out the worst crash the financial world will ever experience, twenty years later you'd have made money. (See why we want a generous emergency fund? We never want to risk having to sell in a panic, after a drop in the market. We need time to let our money come back to us, as it always does.)

History shows that, on average, money properly and semi-conservatively invested in a diversified assortment of stocks will double every 7.2 years and approximately triple every ten years.

This is big. It's major! Does it seem too good to be true? Well, it's been true for generations. It was true through the Great Depression and two world wars, so it's probably going to continue to be true. As I write what you're presently reading, the market has been a bit stagnant due to factors I happen to understand but which are a bit beyond the scope of this particular book. Suffice to say we may be looking at less-impressive returns for a number of years going forward, but that's the short term. In the long run, I confidently expect the market to do what it has always done.

The Man keeps a lot of his money in the stock market. He does this because he's greedy, and he wants to turn his money into more money. And he knows all about what I've discussed above. He knows that this is how the rich get richer. Is that our objective? I say no, not really. I'll quote a song that will appear on my *Back to School* CD I'll be releasing in the next few months. The song existed before this book, and is called "Me Against the Man." In a way, this song has guided my entire road to financial independence.

I don't want to be The Man
But if I can
I'll get out of his clutches

Rip me off a miracle
I'll pull the wool
Over while he watches

He won't see what's coming
Until the referee raises my hand

Place your bets on me against The Man

We don't have a zillion dollars to turn into several zillion more dollars, but we don't want or need all that. We just want to learn from the strategies employed by The Man, so we can adapt them for our own purposes. We want to get out from under that dude's thumb so we can fully enjoy the rest of our lives in reasonable comfort and security. That's all we want! Investing allows us to continue living our lives as we're already living them, while making steady progress toward financial independence and lives that are even better. So let's do it! Let's talk about how we can make our money work for us, turning itself into more money.

Investing Basics Interlude: Pieces in the Total Return Puzzle

Before we dive into the different types of investment accounts and the order in which I recommend prioritizing them on the path to financial independence, it may be helpful to quickly talk about the big puzzle we call *total return*, and the various puzzle pieces we get out of the investing puzzle box. Once we throw our money into stocks (and perhaps bonds, which I don't currently recommend for reasons I'll cover in detail later), that money earns us more money (eventually, if we've invested wisely) in various ways. Here are the puzzle pieces:

Appreciation of stock price. This one is quite simple. Say we decide to buy ten shares of Microsoft at $50 per share. If the price of those shares goes up to $60 per share over the next few years, we've made $10 per share or a total of $100. These dollars earned are capital gains. They are taxed at a rate lower than that of normal income, and this is nice for us. Importantly, these gains are only on paper until we decide to actually sell our shares. We don't pay any capital gains taxes unless we sell.

Dividends. Many (but not all) publicly-traded companies will pull out a portion of their profits each quarter and distribute a dividend to their shareholders. General Motors, for example, pays a generous annual dividend of almost 5% (for the sake of simplicity, we'll assume it's exactly 5%). This means that every year, if we own $1000 in GM stock they'll send us $50, or $12.50 per quarter. This is our money to keep (nice!) but we have to pay taxes on it (not nice!). Fortunately the taxes are minimal for the "buy and hold" investor and can actually be zero under certain circumstances (living frugally has tremendous tax advantages…..low expenses, low income needed, low taxes) and in certain states. My strategy includes concentrating most of my high-dividend payers in tax-advantaged accounts until retirement looms (more on this nuance later).

Other Distributions. Certain types of investments result in distributions that behave kind of like dividends (and may actually be called dividends), but are taxed differently. I generally recommend steering clear of such complications, especially while learning, because keeping things understandable and relatively simple is central to my plan. One exception I make, in my tax-advantaged Roth IRA, is Real Estate Investment Trusts or REITs (which can be purchased individually or as part of a fund). These can pay super-high dividends (I hold two that pay more than 12%) while also offering the possibility of appreciation in the stock price, but the dividends are taxed as normal income. Jumping into REITs also subjects one to the whims of the real estate market (but, for me, is more relaxing than actually owning real estate!). Distributions on bonds are also taxed in different ways, and can be tax-free depending on your state and which bonds you purchase. I'll spend very little time discussing bonds because I'm a non-fan of them, especially for the long-term investor (like us), at this time.

Really, you can think of your investing puzzle as consisting of just stock value appreciation and dividends earned. Should you decide to invest only in stock mutual funds and not individual stocks (highly, highly recommended for the beginner) you'll only have to keep track of two puzzle pieces. Even a child can handle putting together a puzzle that consists of just two puzzle pieces, right? We can do this!

End of Investing Basics Interlude. Now let's dig deeper.

Where Should I Put My Money?

We'll start by discussing the basic types of investment accounts that are available, then do a little diving into the specifics regarding what has worked for me and how I recommend allocating money among and within these accounts. You may need to let some of the complicated stuff kind of float over your head during an initial read-through, then come back to it later once things start to click. (Don't panic! I've had to do this every time I've read something new on the topic of finance.)

The order in which these types of accounts should be prioritized is greatly dependent upon an individual's personal financial situation, stage of life, particular goals, and short- and long-term tax strategy. In my strong opinion, it is not at all necessary to be precise with the order in which these are prioritized, or to stick with that order as life events alter financial needs and priorities. You'll want to get close to the optimum allocation, but I don't believe it's necessary to be perfect. It will all be your money, and it will all be earning you more money; you'll just want to estimate when you'll need each stockpile of these dollars later, and where you'll want various amounts so you can access the funds without wasting a sizable portion on unnecessary taxes and/or early withdrawal fees.

Before you got to this point, you wiped out all debt costing you more than 5% and you are maintaining an appropriate emergency fund, right? Okay, good. Now you truly are ready to invest.

In general (remember, your specifics may suggest something different), I recommend directing savings into investment accounts in the following order:

1. 401k up to employer match.
1a. 401k above employer match (to max) if plan offers solid investment options.
2. Traditional IRA if workplace 401k investment options are crappy.
3. HSA if available.
4. Roth IRA (to max).
5. Taxable investment account.

Let's dig into some details regarding what each of these types of accounts is, and why I recommend them in this particular order. I started at the anticipated end (trying to make sure I'd have enough money to last me to the grave) and increasingly put my savings to work to cover anticipated living expenses closer and closer to the near future. Once I was reasonably certain I had myself covered all the way from eventual death back to the present, I was ready to declare financial independence. How did I do this? Let's see.

Last Things First: 401k Plans

If your employer offers a 401k plan, this is likely where you'll want to direct your first chunks of investable savings now and throughout your working years. I say "last things first" because this is the money you'll end up wanting to withdraw last, when you're in your sixties, seventies, and beyond. This is the "set it and forget it" part of the plan, except you won't truly want to "forget it" because you'll want to regularly consider upping the percentage of your paycheck splitting into this investment account (more on that shortly) and you may want to adjust the type of funds you're using as you get older (more on that later as well). We start here not only because the 401k offers great tax advantages, but because you may have the option to take advantage of an employer "match." For example, if your company offers a match of 50% up to 5% of your income, for every $100 you contribute to your 401k they will throw in an extra $50 up to the point at which you're contributing more than the first 5% of your salary. This is free money! If you found fifty bucks on your front porch, would you just leave it there? No, of course not. Take the money! It's yours forever, and it's like automatically earning 50% on your investment. *Do not leave free money on the table.*

Employers offer varying 401k "match" programs. These can run the gamut from fantastic to shamefully bad. At my first real job out of college, I got a 100% match with no limit (should have contributed more to take better advantage of that, darn it). Some employers don't offer any match at all. If you work for one of these and you're not extremely happy, I'd suggest considering a job switch; such selfishness probably transfers to other areas and will rear its ugly head eventually. Most reputable companies offer some sort of match. Take the free money!

The tax advantages of a 401k are plentiful, and end up making a big difference in how much money you'll have to fund your golden years. Your contributions to this type of account are pre-tax. Before any tax deductions come out of your check, your 401k contribution (including what you'd otherwise pay in taxes) zips over to your retirement account where that extra chunk of money can earn more money and you won't have to pay taxes on it until you withdraw the cash later in life. Rather than making nothing on money you gave the government, you're earning (to put it simply) "interest" on that money, then interest on the interest, year after year. Bonus: living wisely and sensibly (as you will if you take my advice from this book), you'll likely be in a lower tax bracket later in life and will pay less in taxes than you would have paid during your working years. Also, because your 401k contributions are pre-tax, you'll be lowering your taxable income *now* as well, paying less in taxes at present and in the future.

You'll definitely want to prioritize your 401k if your employer offers a match, and contribute a percentage of your income that gets you the entire match that's available. Beyond that, you'll probably want to contribute more because of the great tax advantages. The possible exception? If your employer offers a really bad 401k that offers only funds that will minimize your earnings and force you to pay fees that eat you alive. We'll get into specifics on this later, and I'll help you figure out how to know if this is the case. If you're stuck with a crappy 401k, you may want to just get the match and put any additional money into your own separate "traditional" IRA.

401k contribution limit, 2016: $18,000 (under 50), $24,000 (over 50).

More Last Things First (Maybe): Traditional IRAs

If your workplace 401k options stink, consider only contributing enough to get the employer match and stopping right there. Then you can take after-tax dollars and start a separate traditional IRA (Individual Retirement Account) on your own. (We'll get into how you set up these accounts in just a bit. It's pretty easy.) You'll miss out on the pre-tax advantage on the front end, and you'll end up paying taxes on the back end just on the extra money your investments have earned for you. Some good news? You'll be able to deduct your contributions to this account on your current-year taxes (with some limitations based on income, which probably won't affect most who happen to be reading this book), and reduce your tax bill. More good news? You'll be able to invest your money in good, inexpensive, efficient funds and not waste money due to your employer's poor choice of 401k providers.

My employer offered a great 401k, so I loaded my money into that account and never opened a traditional IRA. I think an employer's plan would have to be quite poor to make skipping the tax advantages a good idea. Also, there are limits to how much one can contribute, in total, to a traditional IRA and Roth IRA per year, and as we'll discuss in a moment I really love the Roth IRA. But in some cases, the employer's 401k plan can, indeed, be nasty and warrant consideration of a traditional IRA as part of the mix.

IRA contribution limit (traditional and Roth combined), 2016: $5,500 (under 50), $6,500 (over 50). Income limits apply; if you're reading this book, it's likely that you aren't anywhere near them.

The Wildcard: Health Savings Accounts (HSAs)

Next, if your employer offers a Health Savings Account (HSA), it's worth considering. I actually failed in this department, because I didn't understand the whole concept until I was already close to retiring. Fortunately Dave has been contributing to his HSA for years and we'll be in pretty good shape in this department.

HSA dollars come out of your paycheck pre-tax, giving you some of the same benefits you get with a 401k. They are usually directed into some sort of very conservative investment bucket, earning a bit of extra money (if not much) over the years you don't use the funds for health care. Importantly, this money (generally your contribution plus extra thrown in by your employer) will be yours forever, to use for health care-related expenses for the rest of your life, even long after you've left that job. Traditional health insurance may make more sense for those who spend a lot of time at the doctor, are saddled with serious health issues, etc. But for the reasonably healthy individual who doesn't run to the doctor every time he or she encounters a runny nose, the HSA can be a great long-term option.

HSA contribution limit, 2016: $3,350 (single), $6,750 (family).

Middle Things in the Middle: Roth IRAs

I love the Roth IRA as an option for the early retiree. In my opinion, this is a great place to park money that will come in handy to cover some expenses during early retirement and, more so, throughout all remaining years of life, providing tax flexibility. Money contributed to a Roth is post-tax (meaning you've already had taxes deducted when you got paid by your employer), but you will never pay taxes on this money *or your earnings* again. Check it out! Your earnings in a Roth IRA are tax-free, forever!

The earnings on your Roth (the money your investments make for you), in my plan, are for life after you turn 59 ½. That's when you'll be able to access those earnings tax-free. But your original contributions (the money you pulled out of cash and put into the account) can be withdrawn after five years from original deposit year without penalty, should you happen to need that money sooner than anticipated. So the Roth IRA offers some nice flexibility, and lovely tax advantages on the back end.

IRA contribution limit (traditional and Roth combined), 2016: $5,500 (under 50), $6,500 (over 50). Income limits apply; if you're reading this book, it's likely that you aren't anywhere near them.

First Things Last: Taxable Investments

A-ha! The exciting and fun taxable investment account! According to my plan, all funds that weren't more appropriately placed somewhere else (covering current expenses, wiping out debt and maintaining the emergency fund, building retirement accounts like the 401k or Roth IRA to cover later and middle years post-work) spill into this account.

This is the place for the lion's share of money that will cover life expenses during the early part of retirement (with no withdrawal penalties or anything like that), and portions of retirement thereafter as well (because when you succeed, you'll end up with more money than you will ever need and a lot of it will be in your taxable investment account by default, continuing to earn more money for you forever). This is also the place where you may want to start with a simple investment strategy that minimizes any needless tax obligations during the pre-retirement run-up (we'll be getting to that very soon), and begin making changes as retirement approaches.

Taxable account contribution limit: the freaking sky.

What I Say vs. What I Did

Maxing a 401k (contributing the maximum amount allowed by law) is a sound idea. It's highly recommended, actually. However, fully maxing mine didn't make complete sense under my plan, ever, for a couple of reasons. Dave has a separate 401k with a balance even higher than mine, and since we're in this together I increasingly took that fact into account. Also, I could tell years ago that I was on pace to end up with more than enough in my 401k to cover my later years. I consistently increased the percentage I was having deducted for the account because I wanted the tax advantages, but I simultaneously prioritized my other investment accounts so I'd be ready to cover earlier stages of middle-age retirement as well. In case your circumstances are very similar to mine, I'll share my precise investing regimen for the last several years.

1. 401k (gradual ramp-up to 20% of income deducted pre-tax)
2. Roth IRA (maxed)
3. Taxable investment account (all other extra cash)

If I had access to a time machine, I would add an HSA to the mix (and max it) before hitting the taxable account. But once I learned what a good idea this is, I was so close to retirement that I didn't bother. I would also start contributing to a Roth IRA much earlier in life, even if just a little at first to get started. If anyone reading this has a time machine, please let me know. I also threw a little extra cash at my mortgage principle from time to time, mostly just to see how it felt (and in honor of my late mother, who paid an extra $50 on my parents' home loan every month without fail and ended up paying off the house early). Because my mortgage interest rate is low and I'm far outpacing it in the market, I eventually stopped doing this.

Getting Started: Opening Accounts

Opening a 401k should be pretty simple. If your employer has a 401k program, you should already have been walked through the process. If you didn't get into your workplace program and it's an option, obviously you'll want to fix that mistake by contacting your boss or human resources department a.s.a.p. It's rather likely that if you're in a 401k you aren't certain about what, exactly, your money is doing. You may not even know which funds you've selected, or even how much you're contributing, or whether your employer offers a match. Don't feel guilty; this is very common. We'll go over the basics in a bit, and you can give yourself a quick check-up and make any smart adjustments that are necessary. First, let's cover the basics of getting the other various accounts you'll need into existence so we can end up funding those as well.

The day I opened my taxable account, after much research, I was very nervous about it. I got through all steps but the last one, and then stared at the screen of my laptop for a full hour before hitting the "open account" button and depositing money from my checking account. I had been ramping up the savings plan for years at that point, and putting off the investing part of the big plan that I knew I'd have to conquer were I to ever get off the treadmill and win the fight against The Man. My checking account balance had become rather impressive due to all the great economizing, but I was earning nothing on that money. I had researched high-interest (supposedly) online savings accounts and the possibility of using certificates of deposit (CDs) and creating a "CD ladder" to get slightly-higher interest rates, but it just wasn't going to get me to where I needed to go. I knew I had educated myself enough on the topic of investing in the stock market, but it was scary. Finally, I hit the button and initiated the movement of the first $5,000 from my bank (where it was just sitting) to my investment account (where it would earn...something, I hoped?). Done.

So where did I go to do this, and how did I pick an investment company? I went with Fidelity (**www.fidelity.com**). All of my advance research (and there was plenty of it) indicated that, of all the many options, two companies generally offer the best service, information, and fees (and leave everyone else in their dust). A lot of smart people go with Vanguard, a great company helmed by the pioneer of low-cost index fund investing, Jack Bogle. If you're starting from scratch, you may want to consider this route. Fidelity's fees are comparable to Vanguard's, and I prefer their web site, appreciate the way they organize the information I need to make good decisions, and love their mobile app (which I use to check my investments and sometimes make trades from bed before my alarm has even gone off in the morning). Importantly for me, my workplace 401k was already with Fidelity, and I liked the idea of having everything in one place so I could always see my entire picture at one glance.

The process of opening an account with Fidelity was pretty simple. I did everything online, and didn't experience much or any stress or confusion during the simple process. After I prodded him for a year or so (he got started on the plan in earnest a while after I was already rolling and talking about it every day), Dave set up his own taxable account with Fidelity without any assistance from me, and also had no trouble.

Getting Moving: Selecting Funds and Stocks (What Goes Where?)

Though I had done a ton of research on the front end, I made some early mistakes once I started to actually invest outside my 401k. For the sake of clarity, I'll concentrate on what actually did and does work in the context of the larger early retirement plan we're discussing, and try to gloss over the specifics of my own learning curve. In other words, let's see if you can take advantage of the time I've already spent refining this whole process.

I'll guide you primarily in the direction of low-cost index funds. These rule! If you're looking for a low-maintenance and low-cost way to make your savings grow in a tax-efficient manner, and you don't want to be hands-on, you're going to love index funds. As a bonus, they're quite easy to understand and you only have to know about a few of them to figure out which is (or are) best for you. We'll also touch on bonds and bond funds, and why I don't care for them at this time. Then we'll move into territory that's a bit more complicated, and I'll talk about some of my adventures in trading (or buying and holding, mostly) individual stocks, and how wading into this deeper part of the pool can offer additional rewards to those interested in being a little more involved and putting in more time and research in order to customize a portfolio suitable for particular life stages.

For those who really, really want to get into the complicated stuff...no, just kidding. We won't be discussing advanced topics like day-trading (except maybe in passing), options trading, *The Big Short*, or betting on market volatility or...whatever. If I don't understand it (or the tax implications), it won't be covered here. And we won't talk about investing in precious metals or, as I like to call it, wasting your investment dollars because you got scared by conservative pundits on TV and thought you needed some gold in your portfolio. Basically, we're looking for investments that are aggressive enough to get us some great returns, but that also offer enough long-term safety to keep us moving in the right direction without causing a lot of worry. The stock market offers some amount of worry by nature, so let's not add to it, right?

Index Funds

If you look at your 401k plan and the investment options that are available (some of which already hold percentages of your retirement money), you'll see an assortment of *mutual funds* in which your money is invested. These funds get their name from the way they work; many individuals contribute money that goes into a sort of mutual pool, and in aggregate all the money buys an assortment of investments. Each individual investor owns shares in this mutual pool. Perhaps you own shares in some sort of dividend growth fund, international fund, target date fund, government bond fund, blah-blah-blah fund...there may be a bunch of them. There are countless types of mutual funds out there, each managed by someone who is getting a percentage of the money in your account every year in return for managing that fund and buying and selling assorted individual stocks and/or bonds that are part of it. When you're looking at any fund that isn't designated as an "index fund," you may want to consider this statistic:

During an average year, 80% of professional fund managers fail to out-perform the index.

An "index" refers to a simple list of publicly-traded stocks that are part of a grouping of companies that make up the particular index referenced. For example, an S&P 500 Index Fund will hold shares in the 500 largest U.S. companies according to Standard & Poor's (weighted by size, or *market cap*). A Total Market Index Fund will (to oversimplify for the sake of brevity) hold shares in all publicly-traded companies. A NASDAQ Index Fund will hold shares in all companies listed on the more tech-heavy NASDAQ exchange. This makes sense, I think. But why do we care?

The growing, even exploding, trend toward index fund investing or *passive investing* allows the individual investor to buy shares in an index fund and save a boatload on associated fees.   A fund managed by some dude in a tie, or an *actively managed* fund, might carry a fee of half a percent, a full percent, or noticeably more. The S&P 500 index fund that makes up the majority of my 401k carries a cost (known as an *expense ratio*) of...would you care to guess? Okay, I'll tell you. .045%. That's 4.5 one-hundredths of a percent. The dude in the tie would have to out-perform my passive fund pretty noticeably to make it worth my money for me to choose his fund over my S&P 500 index fund. And we have concrete statistics telling us that, most years, *80% of these dudes in ties do not beat the index.* Why should we give them a big percentage of our money? Over decades, this difference in fees can make a difference of tens, even hundreds of thousands of dollars.

As if that isn't enough of a reason to be wary of actively managed funds, they also tend to result in greater tax obligations over the long term. More trading of stocks held in actively managed funds results in more taxable events (when a stock has gone up and is sold at a profit, the profit is subject to capital gains taxes that will end up coming out of your account). The assortment of stocks in index funds only changes (resulting in sale of the actual shares in individual companies) when the list of companies in that index changes. This happens only on rare occasion, so taxes are kept to a minimum.

I hope you're getting the strong impression that index funds are the way to go. If we use history as our guide (and I happen to be comfortable doing this as you know), we see that we have better odds at better results this way, and we can skip actively managed funds altogether. A while back, I moved all of my 401k money out of actively managed funds, including a bunch that I had in one of the oft-recommended "target retirement date" funds at Fidelity. These funds sound good at first, because they take care of everything for the investor, and gradually get a bit more conservative as one approaches planned retirement age. The problem I have with them is that they carry a higher expense ratio, and they underperform my index funds. I have no use for this combo! Once I educated myself, I determined that I can do that money-shifting myself as I get older, and I don't need to pay extra for it. Fidelity's target-date funds aren't bad; I just think we can do better without a whole lot of trouble.

Aspiring early retirees interested in keeping things simple can do just fine investing exclusively in index funds. Many succeed by directing all savings into just one well-diversified index fund.

The right index fund can be a good choice for any of the accounts we've covered. My 401k is all index funds, and my taxable account is about 60% index funds. These days there are plenty of them out there, but I recommend two or three as the most anyone really needs to consider. Fidelity's Total Market Index Fund is the centerpiece of my taxable investment account. You can't really get more diversified than a fund that covers everything, so this one is my general-purpose favorite. (Comments on diversification coming shortly!) A total market fund wasn't an option in my 401k, so I went primarily with Fidelity's S&P 500 Index Fund, and put 20% of my money into an Extended Market Index Fund to pick up some mid-cap and small-cap (or mid-sized and smaller-sized) companies in the next tier and gain a little more diversification. I also have some of each of these funds in my taxable account (in addition to a NASDAQ index fund), largely because I started throwing money into index funds while I was still learning and it didn't make sense to sell out of my index fund assortment later when all of them were showing good performance. If I were starting from scratch, I'd probably stick mostly with the total market fund in my taxable account. If I could get that fund in my 401k, I'd have everything in it right now; as things are, I'm very happy with my slightly-more-complicated, nicely diversified mix. Many smart people recommend holding an international index fund as well, but I'm not sold on the concept as something that's necessary. Many or most large U.S. companies do so much business overseas these days that sticking with domestic stock funds offers a lot of exposure to global markets.

You can find index funds by searching under mutual funds on your investment company's web site, then narrowing your search to index funds only (it's pretty easy on Fidelity's site...once you open an account and fund it, you'll be prompted to decide where you want to put your money and you'll end up at a list of funds). Each fund has a corresponding symbol or abbreviation, sometimes called a "ticker." The fund name changes slightly once your balance gets high enough for conversion to the higher-balance version of the same fund with lower fees, but the underlying stocks remain exactly the same. Here are the official names and tickers that correspond to the index funds I've mentioned. Note that if you go with a different investment company, you'll want to be sure to select the lowest-fee index fund option they offer and the fund will go by a different name than Fidelity's.

Fidelity Total Market Index Fund
Premium Class ($10,000 minimum initial investment), FSTVX
Investor Class ($2,500 minimum initial investment), FSTMX
You could put all of your eggs in this diversified basket, keep it simple, and be fine not complicating matters any further.

Fidelity 500 Index Fund (Covers the S&P 500)
Premium Class ($10,000 minimum initial investment), FUSVX
Investor Class ($2,500 minimum initial investment), FUSEX
The largest 500 U.S. companies tend to pay higher dividends, and your dividend income will be perhaps a quarter or half percent higher here than in the more-diversified Total Market Fund.

Fidelity Extended Market Index Fund (Covers mid-cap to small-cap companies)
Premium Class ($10,000 minimum initial investment), FSEVX
Investor Class ($2,500 minimum initial investment), FSEMX
Dividends in this fund will be perhaps a quarter or half percent lower than in the Total Market Fund. Smaller company stocks sometimes performs better during economic recoveries like the one we're currently experiencing.

Fidelity NASDAQ Composite Index (higher fee, not necessarily recommended)
Single-class fund ($2,500 minimum initial investment), FNCMX

Heavy on tech and health industry stocks that pay lower dividends but may offer faster growth and stock price gains. Most will want to skip this one.

The minimum initial investment amount is something you'll only have to worry about on the front end. Once you save enough cash to buy into funds initially, you can then add more in small increments as you please. For example, once you've saved $2,500 and put that cash into a Total Market Index Fund, when you come up with another $100 a few weeks later you can transfer that money into your investment account and then direct it into your fund. (You only have to meet the minimum to get into the fund initially.)

Diversification in investing refers to spreading your investments over multiple companies and multiple industries (and perhaps over different geographical regions and different types of investments as well) so you're not in danger of being negatively affected more than necessary if a particular company or industry or region gets into trouble. Basically, diversification gives you more safety because you're not putting all of your eggs in one basket. The more I study the markets, the more I believe that when a correction or mini-crash or huge crash is in progress...everything drops, and everything drops a lot. Some sectors and stocks hold up a little better (I had some conservative holdings that didn't drop much during the first phase of "Brexit" panic during the summer of 2016, for instance). But when the markets are dropping and the big-money people are in a panic, diversification can only make so much of a difference. Then later, everything comes back up and everyone can relax again. All that said, I've seen that it's a good idea to strive for diversification, and the associated balance in a portfolio is important.

The index funds I recommend above are all broad index funds, consisting of stocks across a wide spectrum of industries. Each offers diversification, and that's good. Should you want or need to consider funds that are not index funds (your employer's 401k plan may not even offer index funds), I recommend that you spend a lot of time reading about your options and digesting the information. Pay close attention not just to a fund's performance in the past (which isn't necessarily likely to hold in the future), but to the fees the guy in the tie is going to charge you to manage the fund(s) for you. Look for diversification and reasonable fees. Comparison shop! If you see a fee that looks high (approaching one percent or exceeding that amount), raise an eyebrow and keep shopping unless that fund manager is a superstar who *always* creams the index. Remember, it's the modern era and you have access to widely-diversified index funds with fees of almost zero.

I've mentioned these "minimum to invest" restrictions you'll come across on the front end, and they probably warrant another mention. You may find the Total Market index fund or S&P 500 index fund you want but then discover that you need to start with at least $2500. Don't despair, because you have a couple of options. The simple option is to just keep saving until you have that much to invest, and I'd lean toward recommending this strategy. The other option is to go back to the menu of investment options and find the same fund as an ETF, or *Exchange Traded Fund.* These are increasingly popular, and many investors who are not me swear by them. They offer the same mix of companies as you'd find in the index fund, and similarly low fees, but trade like individual stocks (without minimums or transaction fees). You could theoretically just stick with ETFs permanently or get started in an ETF, then later move your money to a standard index fund once you could meet the minimum. I pretty strongly lean toward feeling like all of this is just way too complicated and you'll be better off in the long run if you just wait until you can hit the minimum and do things in what I've found is the simplest manner.

One more note regarding index funds...if you're starting with relatively low dollar amounts, you'll likely find that you're not initially getting that great .045% expense ratio I mentioned earlier, rather one that's slightly higher (a still-excellent .08%, perhaps). Once you're in the game with more dollars, investment companies will reward you with lower fees. How great is this! I remember being delighted the first time one of my index funds popped over $10,000 and Fidelity automatically converted my fund from the smaller-account fee to the lower larger-account fee of .05% (which went down another smidge later when Vanguard lowered their fees and Fidelity responded with their own reduction). Both Fidelity and Vanguard will handle this conversion for you, automatically, with no muss or fuss or tax implications. You won't have to do a thing; it will just happen. Cool!

A Word about Bond Funds

What about bonds? What about bond funds? Conventional wisdom dictates that as an investor gets older, he or she should gradually move more into bonds to create a more stable, conservative portfolio. When you buy a bond, you're basically loaning your money to a company or government, and they pay you interest for the life of the bond. A bond fund pools your money with that of many others and a guy in a tie manages the bond assortment as you get your share of interest payments, like a mutual fund manager oversees a stock fund. In an economic downturn or in periods of market turbulence, bonds should be safer and offer dependable returns, they say. Government bonds are the safest of all, with returns guaranteed by the full faith and credit of the U.S. government. And when stocks are dropping, bonds (according to conventional wisdom and plenty of history) tend to rise. There's something to be said for this. Some recommend that the percentage of bonds in a portfolio should match one's age (if you're 40, you should have 40% bonds, etc.). I've chosen to disregard this mindset as outdated, or at least not properly dated for the present.

Due to much super-complicated (and probably big-picture smart, in my opinion) manipulation of matters involving our entire planet's inter-connected financial systems in the years-long wake of the Great Recession and near collapse of the whole house of cards in 2008, perpetrated and orchestrated by central banks and the invisible ultra-powerful puppet masters at and above that level (cue conspiracy theory theme music here), bond yields are presently very low. Basically, the people who operate at levels *above* The Man are working to encourage a steering of money out of bonds and even safer places like bank accounts and into stocks for the sake of worldwide financial stability and the preservation of The Man's well-being. We can't change this if we don't like it; this is just the way things are. This is The System, like it or not. This is why your bank savings account earns .01% interest and your certificate of deposit at the same bank earns 1% interest; the people in charge want your money doing something other than sitting in the safest place because they need it to keep pumping through the circulatory system of world markets. The best you and I can hope to do is understand this complicated continuum at least a little, and figure out how to make it work for us. It's very likely (if not certain) that bonds will continue to *not* keep pace with the rate of inflation in the developed world for at least several more years. For this reason, I don't believe that long-term money should be in bonds at this time.

As long as inflation is at about 2% and the ten-year U.S. government bond is yielding about 1.6%, I have no use for ultra-safe government bonds. I don't call this safety; I call it missed opportunity to outpace inflation. State and local governments also offer bonds, as do individual companies looking to raise capital (corporate bonds). These can be purchased separately or as part of a fund, and can earn more than federal government bonds. Yield is, generally, commensurate with risk of default on the bonds in question (which results in the investor losing his/her investment, not a risk connected to insured federal government bonds). These days, an intermediate-term corporate bond fund can offer returns that aren't terrible, perhaps 5-6%. One could do worse than directing a portion of a nest egg into one of these bond funds. But the long-term investor who is buying and holding a diversified stock index fund can do better with the same invested sack of cash. I don't see any bond fund as an option better than stocks at this time.

Here's another comment added after the 2016 U.S. election. Bond yields have increased (the numerical examples mentioned above are now a little out of date). The prices of bond fund shares have gone down as yields have increased, and most experts expect inflation and interest rates to rise in the near term. Basically, the trend will probably continue for a while. This said, my thoughts on bond funds remain the same. I gave them a fresh look, and didn't change my mind at all.

Plenty of smart people recommend an allocation of 80% stocks and 20% bonds pre-retirement, and a move to 70% stocks and 30% bonds upon retirement with a gradual move further into bonds later. My research, based on how things work now and are likely to work during the near- and intermediate-term future, indicates that holding a generous emergency fund (so I never have to sell anything while the market is down) and investing in 100% stocks will result in higher returns and, thus, increased security and a better life.

How the Heck Do I Open an Investment Account? I'm Still Intimidated!

This'll be a short paragraph. Don't be intimidated! It's easy. First, build up a nice balance in your checking account (over and above your emergency fund). I had a nice pile of cash on hand when I started, but I was scared to death and got rolling tentatively with my first $5,000 deposit. You can start with more, or you can start with much, much less. Just start. Second, go to the appropriate web site. As mentioned, after much research, I recommend going with either Fidelity or Vanguard because the extremely low fees associated with their index funds leave these two without true rivals. (If you eventually want to do more trading of individual stocks you can beat Fidelity's trading fees, but they're competitive and you really won't want to be tempted to do too much trading anyway, lest you derail your entire long-range plan.) Third, follow the easy-to-locate links to open an account (or accounts if you're opening different types of accounts all at once) and let the web site guide you through the process. If you get lost and confused, you can use the phone number on the screen to talk to a human or you can visit an actual living, breathing person in one of their local offices. But really...it's quite easy. Remember that many people have done this before *you* decided to set up an account, and they kind of have these web sites set up for ease of use. Sit down at your computer when you're alone and have no distractions, plan to take your time, and you'll be fine. I'm sure of this.

Once I Have My Account Open, Should I Try to Time the Market When Buying?

Ah, this is an age-old question. Conventional wisdom indicates that trying to time the market and buy when it's down and about to go up is a thankless task, and may be impossible. And this is called "wisdom" because it's pretty smart, and largely true. I've looked at studies showing that if an investor has a lump sum and throws it all into the market at once rather than trying to wait for the market to drop before taking action, that investor generally ends up doing better over time. It makes sense because the market always goes up in the long run, so time in the market allows our money to make more money for longer. And unless you're a genuine psychic, you probably won't be able to accurately predict precisely when the market is going to drop and allow you to buy more shares with your money once shares are cheaper.

Say you've been building up your cash, and you're fortunate enough to be sitting on $5000 you're ready to invest. If you wait for a day when the market drops 1%, you'll be able to buy your shares "on sale" and end up making an extra $50 when it recovers. But...number one, you have no way to know with certainty that the market won't drop another 1% the next day. Number two, how long were you holding all that cash, missing out on small gains and accumulating dividends? Generally, I go with the majority on this one. It really does make sense to go ahead and get your money into the market rather than complicating matters by holding cash waiting for the best possible day to invest. This is especially true for those just getting started, without the benefit of experience that might lead to a better instinct regarding market tops and bottoms.

That said, at times when I've come into a bit of a mini-pile of cash (like, say, when I've received a bonus at work, or an especially large commission check after a good month), I've held my cash for a few days or a week or so if the market was looking a bit high after a multi-day string of gains. Waiting for at least a minor drop before throwing cash into investments has surely made a bit of a difference for me, and I wouldn't discourage such efforts as long as they don't drag on for weeks or months. Because you do want to get your money into investments. And really, the difference one can make correctly timing the market is fairly minor. Consider a $1000 investment made either before or after the market goes up or down a rather noticeable 1%. The difference? A whopping $10, which me might also miss out on earning if the market goes up 1% while we're waiting for a drop.

Post-2016 U.S. election comment added here. Again, the day you're reading this section may be a good time to consider what's happening in the world before throwing a big chunk of money into the market. Keep an eye on world events that could cause market turbulence.

If we're talking about buying individual stocks, we're telling a different story. But as we'll discuss later, this involves some advanced skills and instincts that are acquired with experience and self-education. Timing the purchase of shares in individual companies is not the same as trying to time the market at large. When buying mutual funds, it's generally a good idea to avoid attempts to "time the market."

How About a Specific Portfolio Recommendation?

Here, specifically, is how I've allocated my own nest egg or stockpile of financial resources right now, at the moment when I'm about to flip the switch and declare financial independence. I'll include brief notes regarding the evolution of my allocation, as life stages made changes appropriate. Once again, it's important to remember that this is the allocation I've determined is best for *me*. Nobody will want to copy my allocation exactly, because each of us lives our own situation with particular wants, needs, resources, and risk tolerance. I also have a financially-responsible spouse with growing piles of money in particular places, and that plays into what's appropriate for my side of things at this time.

Cash. 10% of total. This is the combo of my emergency fund and cash I have on hand to cover everyday expenses. I've let this balloon as retirement approaches, because the first year or two of retirement would be the worst time for me to need to pull money out of investments during a down market. Once I confirm that I don't need more cash than I expect, some of this will move to conservative investments.

Taxable investment account. 45% of total. I've gradually begun to make this account more dividend-heavy and will continue doing so with more gusto once my taxable income is lower post-retirement (when my tax rate will be lower). I'm doing this by moving more into individual higher-dividend stocks, but the same can be accomplished by moving from, say, a total market index fund (dividend around 1.5% or a bit higher) to an S&P 500 index fund (dividend slightly above 2% at present). The effect is more dramatic with individual stocks (I'm shooting for dividends of 3.5 to 4 percent overall in my taxable account, ultimately, and have been selling out of no-dividend stocks gradually as my life stage situation changes and I'll want the cash to live). I let my index fund dividends reinvest themselves in the funds, and let my individual stock dividends flow to cash so I can reinvest manually and rebalance as needed. Some of these dividends will ultimately replace my paychecks.

Total Market Index Fund (FSTVX) – 25%
S&P 500 Index Fund (FUSVX) – 15%
NASDAQ Index Fund (FNCMX) – 10%
Extended Market Index Fund (FSEVX) – 10%
30 individual company stocks selected for diversity/dividends – 40%

Roth IRA. 15% of total. One of my big regrets is not opening a Roth earlier. Because of annual contribution limits, I could only pile so much into this account before retiring, and one must show taxable income to contribute to an IRA. Once it's clear that there will end up being enough in your 401k, I recommend hitting the max on the Roth as early in life as possible. Note: my dividends on this account are roughly 4.5% overall, and I plan to add another REIT (pending the real estate picture at the time) once I build up enough cash in the account later this year. I have my dividends in the Roth set to flow to cash so I can rebalance as needed. I may also gradually roll portions of my 401k into my Roth once my tax liability is lower overall (this from the Advanced Retirement Strategies file...google it after you join me in early retirement!). This account is mostly conservative mega-cap stocks with a few riskier dividend plays.

10 individual dividend growth stocks including one REIT – 100%

401k. 30% of total. Let's be clear; this percentage is a bit low for someone about to retire and no longer be able to contribute to his 401k. You may recall me mentioning that Dave has a healthy 401k, and this plays into my strategies. Also, I ended up saving a lot more money than expected the last few years, and kept pumping it into my taxable account while increasing my workplace 401k deduction percentage gradually once every few months as I kept seeing more extra cash in my checking account. (Fidelity allows an employee to do this online, and it takes about a minute. Your employer never needs to have undue attention drawn to how much of your paycheck you're saving! It's very easy to increase deductions manually in accordance with comfort level and life situations.) I won't be touching this money for more than a decade, so I expect it to triple to fund my later golden years.

S&P 500 Index Fund (FUSVX) – 80%
Extended Market Index Fund (FSEVX) – 20%

Bonus Money!

The accounts I noted above total 100%. But I'm not finished. I also have bonus money!

Home equity. I've mentioned that we have a truckload of equity in our house. This makes the whole situation more relaxing for me. If we eventually decide to relocate to Latin America, we'll sell the house and pocket the cash (tax-free), add it to our existing stockpile, and have about three times as much money as we'll need to live the rest of our lives like kings (allowing for plenty of time to continue learning Spanish, gracias). Or if we encounter some sort of huge financial calamity or just decide we want to put more of our money into investments, we'll have the option of selling our house and moving a few minutes further from town where we could buy a place with cash. Of course there's no guarantee that the real estate market won't crash again, or that Nashville will retain its present status as a super-hot "it" city, so I consider all of this equity a bonus. I've performed my calculations *not* counting what will likely continue to provide a huge safety valve should we ever want or need one.

Social Security and Medicare. If you don't think Social Security will still be solvent when it's time for us to begin collecting, I think you're pretty silly. Nonetheless, I say "good for you." I'm a big fan of calculating early retirement needs considering eventual Social Security checks a bonus. I fully expect to receive Social Security. I can't wait, actually! It will be a lot of fun to already have enough money to cover all expenses, then have more money showing up in the mailbox. By the time I'm old enough to start getting those checks, I'll at last be comfortable enough to begin enjoying some major lifestyle inflation! We may travel more, or buy a pool, or just drink more expensive beer and not worry about it. One or both of us may delay benefits to increase the size of our checks, or not. We'll see how everything looks when we get there. In any event, it'll be super-fun. And when I can hop into the Medicare health plan, I'll hop with great enthusiasm. I'm hoping the enrollment age gets lowered to 50 or 55 so I can hop earlier. The savings won't be huge, but there will be savings (and I so love to save). *Egads! Government health care!* Yes please. I want it. I don't want to debate it, I just want to have access to it. For the sake of those of you who don't like the sound of this, I kind of hope early Medicare enrollment happens but remains optional. I want to compare notes and let you know how much less I'm spending for the same health care. Or if I end up being wrong, I want to be able to switch back!

Another post-election comment added: I guess I won't hold my breath at this time.

Possible inheritance money. My parents both passed years ago. As discussed, I was smart about what I did with a meager inheritance and was able to create a life devoid of debt other than a mortgage, permanently. If you get an inheritance, be smart! Don't blow the money. Use it to pay off any problematic debts, then improve your present *and* future. Dave's wonderful parents are both still with us. There may end up being some inheritance money, or not. Heck, they may outlast both of us and wouldn't that be great. Regardless, we don't consider any possible, eventual inheritance money as part of our financial picture. It's their money, not ours. We'd prefer to see them spend every last cent on themselves, making their own lives as fantastic as possible. They've earned it and they deserve it! I can't see looking at this issue from any other angle. If I had kids, I'm sure I'd want to investigate the tax issues and be sure to leave them a nice inheritance. Since I don't have kids, I hope to spend every last cent of what I've saved before I keel over dead with a smile on my face. Woo-hoo!

So, you now have an example of how one guy has arranged his finances to fund the rest of a lifetime. Each individual's situation is different, so my specifics should really just be considered a little food for thought and perhaps a starting point as you learn and adjust based on your own situation. If you choose to keep things simple, you may want to stick with just index funds (just one of them, even). I don't recommend it, but you may want to lean a bit more toward the conservative side and look into adding bond funds. Or if you want to add a bit *more* risk and you determine that you have an interest in devoting extra time and effort, perhaps you'll want to see if you have a knack for dealing with individual company stocks.

Investing in Individual Stocks

Warning! If a savings account is the kiddie pool and index fund investing is the deep end, investing in individual stocks is the ocean. You're likely to remain pretty safe over the long run if you stay in the pool. There are rip tides and sharks in the ocean, so you'll want to have some valid reasons to do more than just enjoy the view from a distance. Remember, 80% of professionals under-perform the index! These professionals live and breathe the stock market. Are you likely to do better than these guys in ties? Maybe not. Probably not. Okay, almost certainly not.

If you decide to dabble in individual stocks, you had better have valid reasons to do so and be willing to put in the time necessary to succeed. Because you are increasing your level of risk.

All that said, I do it. And I started a little too early. But I know myself, and I knew that I'd need to complicate matters just a bit in order to keep myself fully engaged. I'm a little bit of a gambler, and I wanted to see if I had a knack for slightly-riskier investing (you should consider trying to suppress this impulse if you have it, I think). Hey, I lost a small amount of money I didn't need to lose in the early days, but overall my strategy worked. I made a few mistakes (penny stock down 96% and kept in the portfolio as an eternal reminder to not be stupid, anyone?). I made some money too (tech stock up 100% in a year, anyone?). Crucially, I now hold individual stocks for a specific reason. The reason is a long sentence, so prepare yourself. Because dividend income from my taxable investment account will partially fund my early retirement and I want to continue owning all of my stocks as long as I feasibly can before I start selling them to live on their appreciated value, I've been gradually increasing my anticipated dividend income.

Did you "get" that? If not, try reading it again. It's important enough, and set to work beautifully enough, that it qualifies as a guiding principle. It's a fairly important part of my overall strategy.

As your retirement date draws near, begin gradually adopting a higher-dividend strategy in your taxable account.

Once we sell our stocks (individual stocks or shares in index funds or other mutual funds), they will no longer be able to continue earning money for us. Our dividends will be gone, and if the stock prices go up it won't matter to us because we no longer own those stocks. That's kind of sad, don't you think? I've already mentioned that I hope to spend as much of my accumulated money as possible before I eventually keel over dead (in reality I'll be sure everything goes to Dave if I go first, and we'd both love to leave surprise bundles of cash to surviving friends and family members and also make some nice charitable contributions, but that's not as entertaining to read). I won't feel a need to hold a huge portfolio into my final years. But who knows when death will come calling, right? Let's try to avoid selling shares as long as we can, and prolong the cash flow by living off of our dividends while we continue holding the stocks that are paying these dividends. Ideally, we'll end up not even needing all of our dividend income and we can reinvest some of it into more stock. Fun!

As you may recall, dividends bring a bit of a tax obligation as they are received. This obligation varies by state and by income level. In the early days, my opinion is that you won't really need to worry about this matter. The dollar amounts involved are relatively minor. Later, taxes on dividends are a consideration. Your last few working years are likely to be the time your income is at its highest and your tax rate is commensurate. Once you stop working and your taxable income drops (by design), the tax obligation on your dividends will be a lot less. So waiting to move a bit toward higher dividends until the last year or so of traditional employment (then ramping up the project at the outset of retirement) is a sound idea. It's what I've done in my taxable account.

As a buy-and-hold investor, I receive dividends that are categorized as "qualified." This means that I didn't buy a stock strategically to get the dividend, then immediately sell the stock; rather, I owned the stock for a total of six months on either side of what's called an ex-dividend date (the date on which one must own the stock to get the dividend). Satisfying the six-month requirement makes dividends qualified, and means that they are taxed at a reduced rate. ("Unqualified" dividends are taxed as normal income, at normal tax rates.) For instance, if I'm in the 25% tax bracket, my qualified dividends will be taxed at 15% under current (2016) tax law. If I end up in a lower tax bracket, I may find that I owe *no* taxes on my qualified dividends. As you can see, it can be smart to not try to live off of dividends until one's tax bracket is lower (i.e., after retirement). Money we get to keep instead of sending it to Uncle Sam is extra money, and we do love extra money! I actually enjoy paying my fair share of taxes to help fund stuff our government does to make enjoyment of life possible for all of us. But I'm not interested in paying extra.

Selecting Individual Stocks

I'd like to avoid recommending stocks in specific companies, because specifics can change quickly and I'd hate to steer anyone in the wrong direction if realities change between the time I write this book and the time it's being read. I personally monitor my individual stocks every single day, usually throughout each day, even if I'm on vacation in some amazing place, in case I need to react to something that's happening. If you plan to venture past mutual funds, you should be ready to invest this much time. This is important! If you aren't interested in this much extra work, you may want to proceed to the next section of this book. In case you're still reading...

Generally I like to stay above the fray and not do much buying or selling on short notice, because if I've been smart on the front end I've invested my money in a stock I'll want to keep for many, many years. One of the books I read before I started investing advised planning to hold a stock for at least three years to give the company time to execute its plan. I still think this is a pretty good rule of thumb. Of course sometimes there are specific conditions that warrant quick sale or, more often in my experience, quick purchase of *more* stock when the market has overreacted to news and the shares have dropped in price and are crazy-cheap. If we love a sale in the produce section of the grocery store, we *really* love a sale on stocks. Because we're into saving money, and we're into making our savings turn into more money. Watching for true sales on stocks is an acquired skill and a true art, and it's easy to be wrong. This stuff is for advanced students, and I recommend using only a small portion of the nest egg on such adventures. I always tread carefully when diving into these transactions, but I do sometimes tread if I feel that I know enough to probably get it right.

Just yesterday I had some extra money in my checking account and used it to buy additional shares in an amusement park company that's been part of my portfolio for a couple of years and has gone up about 40% since I first bought the stock. This company pays a nice 4% dividend, is poised for domestic and international growth (which big-money investors who move the stock price always like), and has a years-long history of gradual stock-price appreciation. They had a slightly-disappointing quarter, reflected in the quarterly report shared with investors, and the share price dropped far more than my experience indicated was warranted over a couple of days. I've seen the stock do this before, and it always recovers quickly. And I wanted more of this stock anyway! I waited for the market's herd mentality to take the price to what I felt was probably its low point, then bought my additional shares. Because this stock pays a generous dividend, and historic performance of the company and what my research indicates is likely future performance looked great to me, I added to my position. Note that I had actual, valid reasons to put my money in this particular place. I believe in the company, I got the shares at what my research indicated was a good price, and the dividend factor made the stock fit my current life-stage-related strategy.

I'm sorry to tell you that the example above is rather over-simplified in hopes that it isn't impossible to digest. To get this stock-picking thing right, you'll need to do a *lot* of research. To get it even more right, you'll also need to develop an instinct for what the future is likely to hold. You'll need time to learn which information sources are trustworthy and which are sharing tips or updates designed to make someone *else* money at your expense. You can spend hours every day scouring web sites and watching "experts" on financial news channels like CNBC and Bloomberg (I do this often...who'd have thought I'd turn into that guy); it takes a long time to learn how to separate the information you can use from the information aimed at day-traders or the guys in ties or, sadly, impulsive retail investors who can be manipulated by a press release intended to move the price of shares The Man wants moved that day.

You'll need to understand how the U.S. economy actually works, and how the economies of other countries work, and how they all affect each other, and how all of this is likely to affect your investments. You'll need to know what The Fed does, and why it's important, and how it affects the stock market. You'll need to understand how things like employment reports and housing starts reports and manufacturing updates and consumer confidence surveys and shifts in currency markets fit into the big picture. All of these factors (and so many more) play into how the market in general and assorted subsets of it will move, and directions in which *you* will want to move if you want to do better than you could do by just buying shares in index funds and going about your everyday business while not cluttering your mind with so much detail.

In case you, like me, happen to be up for all of this (it really can end up being kind of fun and interesting, I swear) here are a few very basic guidelines I try to follow when considering buying stock in an individual company initially, and when considering adding to a position. Investment experts, note that I'm oversimplifying a lot here. These are just some of the factors I consider in my continuing effort to fine-tune my portfolio to best fund my particular future, and to outperform the market and my index funds (which has been the case for the last few years, fortunately).

Historic Performance of the Stock, Represented in a Graph. This is where I like to start, and I never hear anyone else talking about this particular starting point. (I don't understand why.) If I'm considering a stock, I look at the way the stock price has moved over the last week, month, year, five years, ten years, and entire history of existence. Because I'm a long-term, buy-and-hold investor, I want to see a pattern of up, up, up. Knowing what the stock is doing lately is good, but knowing how it has performed over many years is what really matters to me. Because I'm investing to fund the rest of my life, not to make a quick score. I want to know that I'll make money, not be somewhat likely to lose some of what I invest. If the company pays a super-generous dividend, I might be willing to accept a long-term pattern of sideways stock price movement because I'm confident I'll consistently make money on dividends even if the stock price doesn't go up a lot. If I get a nice dividend and history shows that the stock price tends to go up over time as well, I'm interested. If stock price shows a years-long pattern of rising and the stock is presently in a bit of a "dip" but my other research shows that the company is still in good shape and likely to continue succeeding, the stock may be on sale and worthy of my attention. And if the graphs leave me feeling totally confused, maybe I should take the money I was thinking about putting into this stock and instead throw it into one of my index funds where I won't have to worry about it!

P/E Ratio. The "P" here is the stock price, and the "E" is the company's earnings over the previous twelve months. "Forward P/E" uses an "E" based on the company's projected or predicted earnings over the *next* twelve months. Generally, I like a P/E of 16 or lower, because historically this is a number that has been considered reasonable and a higher P/E can indicate that the stock is presently overpriced. If the P/E is especially low, it may indicate that the market doesn't have much confidence in the company, perhaps for good reasons. There are many exceptions to my "keep the P/E around 16 or a bit lower" guideline, as observed by me as part of my evaluation. For assorted reasons, auto manufacturers and airlines trade at very low P/E ratios right now. Banks trade at medium-low P/E ratios. Certain quickly-growing tech companies trade at amazingly high ratios because their profits are expected to increase exponentially in the future. Some dependable high-dividend companies trade at ratios that are a bit higher because investors are willing to pay a bit more to get a nice dividend.

Basically, if the P/E is very high or very low, I stop to figure out why before I proceed.

Price/Book Ratio. Very generally, if this number is below one the stock price may be a good deal. If it's a lot over one, it may not. As is the case with P/E, if I see that the price-to-book figure is especially low or high I like to know why before I consider buying the stock.

Debt/Capital Ratio. If a company's debt-to-capital ratio gets too high, big-money investors may begin to run from the stock. Basically, if it starts to look like a company may start to run out of money, the stock price will probably drop. This figure can vary greatly by industry, and sometimes a company may be carrying a lot of extra debt for a good reason. If the ratio looks crazy compared to the rest of a company's industry, I like to know why.

Earnings vs. Estimates in Recent Quarters. Companies will generally try to keep the market's expectations slightly low, then hope to exceed these expectations at least slightly when reporting results each quarter. If a company isn't good at managing the expectations of investors, bad surprises can cause a big sell-off when the market doesn't like what it sees and loses confidence in the company's ability to make money and grow. If results exceed expectations, the share price is likely to rise. I like to see a pattern of quarterly results that exceed what the market was expecting, indicating that the company knows how to manage expectations.

Dividend Yield. If I'm holding or buying a stock partly because I want the quarterly dividend income, does the company send me a nice share of their profits or can I do better? The annual "yield" is a percentage kind of like an interest rate on a bank account. If the yield is 3% and I buy $1000 worth of the company's stock, the present dividend will earn me $30 per year (or $7.50 per quarter). If the dividend is low or if there's no dividend at all, I need to be confident that the value of the actual stock is likely to appreciate nicely as time passes. If the dividend is especially high (I hold a few stocks paying super-high dividends as high as 14%), I may consider a company that grows slowly and may not show a lot of share price appreciation, or that carries a lot of debt, or that may be somewhat risky. I like to hold an assortment of dividend yields that is diversified (some stocks that pay no dividends and put their money into their own growth, some stocks that pay conservative dividends, some stocks that pay very generous dividends)...just as I like my portfolio diversified in other ways. A company that has a history of consistently increasing its dividend earns major brownie points at my house.

Dividend Payout Ratio. Does the company keep enough cash on hand to make it likely that they will be able to continue paying the current dividend and perhaps increase it in the future? Again, there are reasons I'll be fine with a payout ratio that's especially high or low. But in general, I feel calm and optimistic if the ratio is well below 100%, preferably around 50% or lower. If this is the case, I feel like a company is being fair about how much of their profits they're sending to me as dividends, and also being smart about how much they're keeping to invest in future growth (which will cause the share price to increase and make me more money on the back end, when I eventually sell the stock).

Short Interest as % of Outstanding Shares. This one is a little complicated. Basically, I check to see if a lot of traders dealing in the more involved side of investing are currently betting that the company's stock price is going to fall soon, and "shorting" the stock. If this figure is higher than around 2%, I want to think about why this is the case. Sometimes I determine that the goofballs who are shorting the stock are probably wrong, and because of the way shorting works I know that they will have to end up buying the stock soon to cover their shorts. This can mean that it's a good time to buy the stock and gain a little extra appreciation in the share price. But it's easy to get this wrong, so I use the short percentage mostly as a possible warning sign that the goofballs may know more than I do.

Analyst Opinions. What are the guys in ties saying about the company right now? This information is out there, and pretty easy to find thanks to the internet. Fidelity provides a lot of analyst opinion data for most stocks right on their quote page (it's a really convenient place to start). I take what the full-time "experts" are saying into account, knowing that sometimes if everyone is saying I should buy a stock it may be too late because everyone else already bought...and if they're saying I should sell something it may be time to consider buying soon because others listening to these dudes have already sold and the stock price won't be able to go much lower before people sweep in to buy a bargain (raising the stock price).

A Stock's Role in My "Big Picture" Strategy. Fear and Greed are an investor's enemies, and must be avoided at all costs. The fear of losing money can lead one to sell a stock after everyone else has already sold it, locking in a loss when the stock price is likely to go back up later. The greedy desire to make a lot of money at once can lead one to waste resources on a risky stock, or to make other decisions that will jeopardize long-term profits. Because I always keep my own reality, I'm generally immune to Fear and Greed and the dangers of emotional trading. I very strongly recommend setting a long-term strategy, making sure it's a strategy that matches individual long-term life goals, and sticking with the strategy without exception. Before I seriously consider any moves in the market, I step back and take a look at my portfolio and my entire life (seriously!) and confirm that any buying or selling is very likely to keep me on-plan and moving forward. When considering individual company stocks, I also attempt to be sure I'm maintaining adequate diversification in my overall portfolio (i.e., if I already hold two airline stocks, I may not want a third no matter how undervalued they all appear at the time).

Personal Instinct, Backed by Actual Facts. I've kind of developed a knack for picking the right individual stocks for my tailored portfolio. But I'm not psychic. I rely a bit on instinct, but the instinct is tied to actual reality. A company's stock price will end up rising if the company succeeds and grows and shows increasing profits and attracts more and more investors. I look for companies that are well-run and are poised for growth, due to their expertise and/or their place in a changing world. Identifying these companies takes some skills that can only be developed over time. One tip I can offer is my habit of stopping during the evaluation process to ask myself, "Is this company likely to outpace every other company in which I might invest? How likely is this to be true, and why? I have a finite amount of cash; is this the absolute best place for me to put it?"

Personal World View and Moral Code. I'm not a total stickler for avoiding stock in companies I feel are evil. I'm just...a partial stickler. I try to remember that I'm not actually giving money to the people who run companies, rather buying stock from other investors who previously bought the same stock from other investors, etc. (I choose to not shop at certain retail stores because I object to how they operate, but buying stocks is simply not the same thing.) But I do have my limits, and a personal line I don't cross because I know I won't want to root for some companies to succeed and I won't want to hold their stock. For instance, I steer clear of companies that are part of the Military-Industrial Complex because if I owned their stock it would kind of be like I was rooting for the U.S. to go to war so their profits would balloon and the value of my stock would increase. Conversely, I don't buy stock in companies simply because I think they're making the world a better place. I own a lot of stock in what I've determined is the best-run solar energy company in the world. And the stock is presently in the toilet. I'll continue to hold this stock not because I like the idea of clean energy and think we need it to dominate so we can save our planet, but because I expect this particular company to eventually succeed in a huge way. And when it does, I'll make a lot of money on my stock.

So, the factors above are some of what goes into my personal decision-making process as I maintain the roster of individual stocks I choose to buy and hold in my taxable account and my Roth IRA. At this point I do very little selling, because I'm pretty comfortable with the stocks I own and their place in my overall strategy as I enter a new life stage. I do some buying from time to time these days, adding to positions that are most compatible with my present and future and always remembering to keep myself appropriately diversified without too many eggs in one company's or sector's basket. I made most of my bad mistakes back when I was first getting started, and I've held onto a few of those stocks for one of three reasons.

Reasons to Keep Stock-Trading Mistakes in the Portfolio

Yes, there are reasons to keep the nasty dogs in your possession, at least for a while. Huh? Really? Why?

If research indicates that the stock may eventually recover, you may want to wait rather than taking a loss. Any losses are unrealized, or only on paper, until you actually sell stock at a price lower than what you originally paid. If you feel there's no hope, and/or if you determine that what's left of the money you have in a downtrodden stock could earn more for you elsewhere, you'll want to go ahead and realize the loss by selling your shares.

If the remaining value of the stock is so low that it's virtually meaningless, you may want to consider holding the stock in case a miracle occurs. Early in my adventures, I spent about $400 on a penny stock. Please DO NOT waste your time or money on penny stocks (basically, stocks valued at less than a dollar per share). There's a reason they're penny stocks. I made an impulse buy after doing very little research and dreamed of getting rich quickly, and of course lost almost all of my money. The value of those shares is presently about $10. (Oops!) I keep them partly because it would cost me $7.95 to sell them so why bother...partly because who knows, maybe a miracle will happen and I'll still get rich (I'm not expecting this to happen)...and mostly because I like having this holding at the bottom of my list of stocks as a permanent reminder to always do plenty of research before investing in a company, and to never, ever buy penny stocks! If you ever think about buying a stock priced at less than, say, $5 per share...you might want to stop and ask yourself if you're being stupid. There are some decent stocks priced at less than $5, but not many.

If you determine that you'll definitely want to unload shares at a loss, you may want to sell them strategically and take advantage of a *tax loss harvest* during an appropriate tax year. We've discussed that selling shares of stock at a profit (when they aren't in a tax-exempt Roth IRA) results in capital gains on which you'll owe taxes. Conversely, selling shares of stock at a loss counts against any profit you made during that tax year. So if you're sitting on capital gains or anticipating realized profits before the end of the year, it may be a great idea to unload losing stocks during that same year to reduce your tax liability. For example, say I determine that I'm holding too much of nicely-profitable Stock A and I decide to sell some of my shares, registering a capital gain of $500. Rather than paying capital gains taxes on that profit, I can sell shares of my hopeless Stock B that were an old mistake and have lost $600. I've *harvested my loss* and I'm now showing a loss of $100 overall, and I won't owe *any* capital gains taxes. (Unfortunately the government won't feel sorry for you and send you a refund when you show a loss, so getting your capital gains taxes to zero is the best you can do.) Note that mutual funds, including index funds, usually register some capital gains by the end of each year due to changes in the lineup of stocks in the underlying funds. Even if you think you aren't going to register any capital gains during a year, if you hold any funds it's likely that you will and might benefit from a small tax loss harvest if you're sitting on any dead shares. Note: your investment company will keep you updated regarding your year-to-date capital gains via monthly reports.

Taxes? Oh Gosh. Taxes! How Will I Prepare My Tax Return?

One of the reasons I first opened my taxable investment account during the month of March was my tremendous fear of eventually having to deal with a much more complex tax return. I figured I could ignore my concerns for a year or so, and just figure it out by April 15 of the following year. Because I work out of a home office and also have some side income from my singer/songwriter ventures, my taxes were already somewhat complicated. I'd gone to a reliable tax professional for years, and had only recently switched to handling online prep on my own (once I knew what to expect and how to maxlmize deductions without help). *I'll just call Angie*, I told myself. *She'll handle it for me.*

Imagine my horror when I tried calling Angie and discovered that she had disappeared. Oh no! I had a 25-page printout of tax information from Fidelity packed with all kinds of stuff I found completely unfamiliar and mystifying, and my tax lady was not around to tell me what it all meant! I decided to go ahead and try the online tax prep site I'd used for a couple of years, then find a new tax person to help once I confirmed that I was totally lost.

I use H&R Block's web site. It's quite intuitive and easy to navigate, but my new investing situation left me less than optimistic. I went ahead and got started, following the on-screen instructions and providing all the "normal" basics. Then I got to the question about whether or not I had any income from investments. *Here we go*, I thought. *This is where it all goes to hell*. I clicked the "yes" button, selected Fidelity from the drop-down menu of options when the screen asked for my investment company, and held my breath.

Next, the program asked me, "Would you like us to automatically download your investment tax information directly from Fidelity? Enter username and password." *What? Seriously? There's no way it can be this easy.* I did as directed, and about ten seconds later my screen indicated that I was all set and could continue with my return.

Once I was finished with my taxes, I checked the forms before filing electronically. Everything was there, and perfect. I saw capital gains and losses, and my dividend income. In a beautiful twist, I didn't even owe any extra taxes! I got lucky that first year, when I didn't fully understand what I was doing, and happened to not create any extra tax burden at all. Hooray!

The moral of this story is that if you already use a decent tax person, you'll receive the proper tax documents from your investment company and you can take them to your tax prep session along with the other paperwork you always take. If you do your taxes yourself online at any of the top sites, you should be able to click a few buttons and let the appropriate information automatically flow to where it needs to go. It's surprisingly, shocking easy!

Investment Section Wrap-Up

Okay. That was a pretty big splat of information regarding investing or, more generally and accurately, turning saved money into more money. Confused? Hopefully you are. I tried to keep things fairly simple and leave some stuff for you to learn on your own as you advance along the path. But even from the lower floors this skyscraper, by nature, looks tall. If it were super-easy to get to the higher floors, everyone would hop on the elevator and beat The Man with no trouble. The whole system would probably collapse, and we'd need to come up with some other strategy. So if you find all of this overwhelming, be glad! The fact that most people never take the time to figure out how this works is the reason that it's possible. If you've made it this far and you're still reading, I have complete faith in your ability to succeed. Seriously...if I could do this, so can you.

The "saving" part is what's most important. Once you evaluate your life and separate your wants from true needs, then rank *achieving financial independence* above everything you "want" less than that, you *will* save increasingly large piles of cash. Once you've eliminated expensive debt and created an emergency fund, it's time to put your growing savings to work so the dollars can turn themselves into more dollars and eventually fund your enjoyment of financially independent life. How badly do you want this?

I really wanted it. So I figured out how to get it. Succeeding at this plan has been like a lot of things in life; if it looks really complicated and difficult and overwhelming but the end-goal is categorized as *definitely worth it*, why not just jump in and make it happen? I figured that if other people had succeeded, I could too. And now I figure that if I could do it, so can you!

THE SOLUTION, PART 3:
RETIRING

Because I haven't actually pulled the retirement trigger yet and won't officially do so until the very day this book becomes available for public consumption, much of this section will be based on conjecture and advance research. I've done plenty of the latter to be reasonably sure I'll be ready for the next, glorious stage of life not just financially, but also emotionally and physically. Ensuring that the money to fund all remaining years will be stockpiled in the right places in the right amounts is crucial, of course. A nest egg of appropriate size is a required element, as is preparedness to adjust investments appropriately as later life stages necessitate. But why bother going through all the trouble to beat The Man and escape his clutches if anything other than tremendous happiness is waiting in the free expanses on the other side?

We'll talk about how much saved and invested money should be where, and what adjustments will be smart as time passes, in a bit. But first let's dip a toe into the early retirement pool and see if we can make sure the water is as refreshing as it looks before we dive in head-first. I always think it's important to be moving *toward something better* in life, something more fulfilling or satisfying or worthwhile, rather than just trying to escape something unpleasant. Retiring early is a huge undertaking not just on the front end (getting to the point at which it's possible), but perhaps even more so once a new type of life is at hand. We'll want to be as certain as we can that all the effort was worth it.

True Identity and the Core of Being

Time and again, while moving toward achievement of my early retirement goal, I've said both silently and out loud, "I'm so looking forward to being *me* again." Some personality types, like the infamous Type A, are well-suited for the standard American way of life. *Work hard, play hard! Keep up with the Joneses! He who dies with the most toys wins!* This isn't me. I've had to increasingly fall into the "work hard, play hard" thing to survive as I've aged, but this definitely clashes with my picture of a healthy life. While my natural tendency is to expend maximum effort toward the fastest possible completion of anything I attempt, I'm not really psychologically constructed for the pace at which I've been constantly dashing for so many years. I've proven that I can handle it, but I hate it. In refusing to fail anyone, or at anything, I ended up temporarily failing myself. I ended up with a life full of tremendous wonderfulness I haven't been capable of truly enjoying because I left myself completely exhausted. This is about to change.

I'm completely at peace with my decision to stick it out, survive some of my maximum earning years in a job I knew I could do well for reasonably adequate financial compensation, live through the most difficult final years of sacrifice in the wringer, and finally declare victory somewhere between "comfortable" and "wealthy." Will I ever be what people in the developed world consider ultra-rich? Gosh, no. (I hope not, actually, because I'll just feel guilty.) Do I care? I most definitely do not. All along, I've only wanted to create a financial situation that will allow me to be *happy* for my remaining years while I'm likely to have enough of those years remaining to feel like I've lived a full, useful, and enriching life once I croak. This leads us to a very important guiding principle:

The end goal is not money, rather happiness. Once you've accumulated enough of the former to ensure adequate funding of the latter, it's time to declare financial independence.

But what is "happiness," after all? The answer is different for each individual, obviously. I've spent a lot of time, over many years, delving into this issue so that I might make my way to my own happiest possible life-spot. It ends up being not a matter of deciding what I want to *do* during my life, rather a larger matter of who I want to *be*. And as far as I can tell, the *do* part can be organized to make the *be* part possible and eventually very likely.

Back in college, in both business and psychology classes, I was exposed to what I assume is still considered a standard and pretty smart diagram explaining what a human might consider a path to maximizing personal potential. The diagram is in the shape of a triangle, with basics at the bottom and the ultimate success at the top. It's called *Maslow's Hierarchy of Needs*. Essentially, we're supposed to start by satisfying the basic needs like food and shelter and clothing and sex and such. Then we work our way toward the top, and if we're really, really good at life we reach the pinnacle: self-actualization. This means that we've totally kicked butt in life and become the best possible version of ourselves. As a youngster, I remember pondering all this and thinking, "Man, how cool will it be if I can end up self-actualizing! That'll be so cool!"

It's a pretty lofty goal. I don't know what percentage of us even get close to realizing it (it's probably pretty low), but I've kept the faith during ensuing decades and I've still got my eye on that prize. Had I been stuck working for The Man until traditional retirement age, I'm sure I would never have made it. I don't even think I could have remained alive to see the end of that nightmare. But now that I'm getting out early, I'm confident. I am *so* going to self-actualize. That's what I have planned for the rest of my life, anyway.

I'm starting with a general idea of what I plan to *do*, so that I can end up being the self-actualized human being I always hoped to eventually *become*. The rough plan goes back to the core of who I am as an individual, and what has always brought me the most genuine satisfaction. And it's pretty simple. Once I have that arduous "working" stage behind me, I plan to spend one third of my available time concentrating on each of three activity categories. When people find out I'm about to stop working, they often ask, "Really? What in the world are you going to do with yourself if you don't have a job? How will you spend all that time?" I have the answer, and it's this:

1. Creating things.
2. Making the world a better place for humans and animals.
3. Enjoying cocktails.

To clarify, I don't actually plan to spend one third of my waking hours getting drunk. In this plan, "cocktails" are the equivalent of general leisure hours (some but not a majority of which will likely be spent sipping mojitos and/or margaritas). I'm fortunate (very) to be hitched to a significant other whose company I enjoy more than I can even express, and to be surrounded by the coolest group of people I could ever hope to call friends. I look forward to hanging out with these great people, and meeting new humans on my path. I can't wait to travel more, work on my Spanish, get back into working out in earnest (with the side-benefit of reducing health care expenses), hike new trails and enjoy the outdoors, and get to dozens upon dozens of home maintenance projects I've been too worn out to tackle. I may even take up dusting. Oddly enough, I'll consider monitoring and adjusting my investments a leisure activity as well.

The "creating things" part will primarily entail me writing tunes and recording/releasing records (my favorite thing to do) and playing live shows when I feel like it, and writing books (my newer, other favorite thing to do) when I feel like doing that instead. I don't have kids and I'd like to feel like I left a part of myself to remain on the planet when I'm gone. This accomplishes that.

The "make the world a better place" part will involve me giving back, watching for and grabbing opportunities to make lives better.

I feel like my contributions in this area have been woefully inadequate to date. Writing a check now and then or adopting one needy animal at a time or helping the random person with this or that when I have time? That's kind of sad, and simply not enough. I so look forward to having the time (gasp) to fix it, do some volunteering, and be a better person.

I have lists of specifics ready to fill the time I've spent working, once that time is officially mine again. From what I've read in many testimonials and learned by talking with other early retirees, I gleam that having specific plans is a great idea. Whether we enjoy or just tolerate or violently hate our jobs, we spend a lot of time and energy on our work and it's natural that what we do in the workplace becomes a large part of our personal identity. From the CEO to the dude who cleans the bathrooms, and from the influential worker in a small business to the drone serving as a small cog in a giant corporate machine, we all have a role to play and we play it during the majority of our waking hours. One of the first questions one person asks another upon meeting is usually, "What do you do?" What we do tends to become a big part of who we are. And once we're no longer doing it, no matter how much we looked forward to *not* doing it anymore, a void will naturally be created. Creating a new and improved self-identity will be a blast, but it's important to know with some degree of accuracy what, precisely, will fill this void.

Be aware of emotional challenges likely to arise when you exit the working world, and know how you'll fill the natural void before you encounter it.

I recently met a delightful couple who retired the previous year in early middle-age. One stopped working a few months after the other when the wife's last surviving parent died, unfortunately, and left a sizable inheritance. They met with a financial advisor first, confirmed that they didn't really need to keep working if they didn't care to do so, and decided to spend more time with each other and their kids rather than living as they'd been living. Both husband and wife had big smiles on their faces as they shared their story, but they made it clear that they had gone through a definite "adjustment period" and were just coming out the other side.

The husband mentioned that he always enjoyed his job handling maintenance and renovations at a high-rise residential property. "The hours became way too much and I hated the commute," he said, "but after I quit I really missed doing work that I enjoyed." I got the impression that he kind of floundered for several months and felt like he wasn't accomplishing anything. But he figured out how to fill the void by volunteering for Habitat for Humanity, doing work he could enjoy doing well while making the world a better place for people in need. His face glowed as he spoke of his new place in life. Both spouses smiled almost constantly the entire afternoon, and I loved seeing a real-life success story. "I'm totally putting you two in my book," I told them.

Personally, I've chosen to skip the adjustment period and be ready to fill any void I experience right off the bat. I'm ready. I even have a loosely-set daily regimen I'll be ready to follow once I take a few weeks to relax and unclench my brain and soul. I'll still set my alarm (because I love, love, love to sleep and I don't want to miss a bunch of my improved life), check my investments from bed (because for some reason I categorize this as not just useful but also fun), then get rolling. I'll begin by enjoying the long-lost luxury they call "breakfast" (haven't had time for that in years!), then spend 10-15 minutes improving my Spanish, then work out or walk or hike. Some afternoons will be spent working on music or in-progress book ideas, others turning our home into a more pleasant living environment. Evenings will entail hanging out with Dave and our dear friends, with the option of doing other things like, say, playing music in this city where it's always an option if you don't feel the need to get paid for it. Once I'm no longer completely exhausted at the end of every day, I'll be able to do more of what I find fulfilling. In time, I'll seek out volunteering options and continue to expand my personal definition of *a good and satisfying life*. Wow. I can't wait.

I have no interest in "doing nothing." I've sacrificed for years so that I can do things other than what I've *had* to do in order to make ends meet and eventually fund the rest of my life. If I chose to just sit around and relax and get fat, I'm sure I'd fall into a vat of depression very quickly. As stressful as my working years have been, they've provided not just money but also a sense of importance, accomplishment, and (bittersweet) satisfaction. I'll still need what working has provided, except for the money. And my plan is to get these things, in great amounts, using methods of my choice. I'm fairly certain that the work on the front end will be well worth it once I have the freedom to rearrange my daily existence.

Of course I'll still need to keep an eye on the financial side of things. I can only imagine the trauma I'd experience if I had to go back to work involuntarily after plotting and executing my escape! Fortunately I've taken care to be reasonably certain this will never happen.

The Number

The topic of how to determine The Number, or precisely how much one should have in savings and investments before declaring financial independence, is oft-debated. Bring up this topic in an online forum and the argument will rage indefinitely. There are many opinions, and they vary wildly.

One of the most popular and most enthusiastically embraced rules of thumb centers on the 4% "safe withdrawal rate," or SWR. After intensively studying more than a century of stock market history and crunching the numbers, very smart people have determined that one can safely withdraw 4% of a total investment stockpile to fund year one of retirement, adjust that amount annually to account for inflation, and expect to never run out of money. According to this rule, if you determined that you needed $24,000 per year to cover your retirement, you'd know that The Number for you would be $600,000 (4% of which is $24K). If you needed $40,000 per year, The Number would be a cool one million bucks. (Perhaps you've just noticed how much less you'll end up needing to retire once you've cut the fat out of your annual budget! Might want to re-read the first section of this book...!)

Studies have shown that even when retiring at the worst possible time (like, say, September of 1929), the 4% SWR worked. And, importantly, this concept assumes no additional influx of funds from any other source, including Social Security. For this reason, I feel comfortable going with an SWR of at least 5%. As mentioned, I plan to create a bit of income here and there, and I have complete faith that I'll be receiving some sort of Social Security benefit (plus I have all that home equity I can tap in case of emergency, and Dave will continue working for a while as our investments continue to grow largely untouched). Of course there are pessimists out there who look at current market conditions and think that a 3% SWR makes more sense. The "S" in SWR stands for "safe," and I'm completely in favor of each individual determining what that means.

If you want to go with the standard 4% safe withdrawal rate, you can easily estimate how much money you'll need to cover a year's expenses and multiply it by 25. If your situation and beliefs are more in line with mine, multiply by 20. This, for you, is The Number. And now you have an official goal! Remember to be flexible in regard to this dollar amount. And remember that the further you presently are from retirement, the more flexibility you'll need. Things change, and your projections will need to go up and/or down accordingly. My number dropped dramatically over the last few years, as inflation remained low in the U.S. and my cost of living kept going down due to lifestyle changes. But the opposite can be true as well. The closer you get to retirement, the more accurate your calculations become.

To determine The Number, multiply projected annual expenses by 25. Assuming a Safe Withdrawal Rate (SWR) of 4% per year, this is the total stockpile you'll need to be reasonably sure you'll never run out of money. Adjust up or down based on individual circumstances and comfort level. Smart lifestyle adjustments may allow you to retire on much less.

Many aspiring early retirees calculate The Number and choose to stick to it without flexibility. This may not be a bad idea, and can guarantee there are no "OOPS! I quit working too early!" risks. I came up with two numbers here, one for Dave and me combined so I'd know what we'd really end up needing in total, and one to cover just my half of things so I'd have a motivational personal goal. Do what works for you!

I also came up with separate sets of numbers in case we decided to relocate outside the U.S. so we could get out of the rat race earlier and simultaneously. As mentioned, this was kind of an obsession of mine for a while and to some extent still is. I've loved four fact-finding missions to Latin America, and if Dave ever comes home from work one day and says, "I'm sick of this! Let's get the hell out of here!" I'll be ready to start packing (and trying to get all of our dear friends to join us immediately). Such a move isn't imminent, and we've decided to let the concept sit on a back burner in case we determine with certainty that we have a real taste for it later. In addition to lovely people, awe-inspiring landscapes, iguanas and/or monkeys, and a total lifestyle evolution I'm pretty sure I'd love, such a move would offer a dramatically lower cost of living. The Number for us to both cease working and live like kings for life is much lower in this scenario, and we surpassed it about two years ago. It's good to know that these international options will now always be available.

For the sake of those who might be intrigued, let's discuss it in a little more detail.

Beyond the Border: Going LCOL or AWOL

One option for the retiree attempting to stretch a nest egg is to make those dollars go further by moving from a high cost-of-living (HCOL) area to a low cost-of-living (LCOL) spot somewhere else. From state to state and region to region here in the U.S., the cost of things tends to be a function of income level in each particular place. In parts of the country where people are getting bigger paychecks, life costs commensurately more than in places where paychecks are smaller.

A 2016 Regional Price Parity study by the Bureau of Economic Analysis covered in the *New York Times* compared the relative value of $100 based on the regional cost of basics like food, shelter, utilities, gasoline, taxes, etc. The difference from one state to another is somewhat striking.

Least Expensive U.S. States (Relative Value of $100)
Mississippi ($114.30)
Arkansas ($114.30)
Alabama ($113.90)
South Dakota ($113.60)
Kentucky ($112.70)

Most Expensive U.S. States (Relative Value of $100)
District of Columbia ($84.70)
Hawaii ($86.40)
New York ($86.40)
New Jersey ($87.30)
California ($89.00)
Maryland ($90.70)

For the retiree living off of savings and investments, income is basically set (or "fixed") and moving from one region to another won't result in a higher or lower influx of funds as it would for the working person. The accountant relocating from California to Mississippi and landing a similar accounting job could expect a noticeable decrease in salary and might not experience an improved financial situation. But the retiree making the same move has no such concerns, because his or her investments will be performing identically regardless of where he or she chooses to live.

Before deciding that an LCOL state is a major bargain, however, a retiree should check out the state taxes. Different states tax capital gains and dividends at different rates (some not at all). Tennessee, for example, has traditionally levied a 6% tax on dividend income above a certain level, but is in the process of phasing out this tax entirely at a gradual pace, lowering it 1% every year starting in 2016. Other states that harbor a large number of retirees maintain relatively high taxes on investment income to bring in the money needed to fund services for this population (which isn't contributing income taxes). Every state needs money to fund its services, and every state goes about getting this money from taxpayers using its own combination of taxes. The retired individual interested in maximizing the nest egg can, without too much trouble, research tax policies in target states and figure out which is a good financial landing spot. I'll use my current home state to illustrate this point.

I've mentioned that Tennessee is in the process of phasing out its dividend tax. I'm sure you know that as an investor I like this very much. Additionally, the state has no state income tax and (in all regions, as far as I know) relatively low property taxes. Instead, Tennessee makes up its revenue shortfall with a sales tax that is one of the highest in the U.S. There's even a sales tax on food. (I'm opposed to this from an economical, philosophical, and moral standpoint because it's a regressive tax that affects poor people the most and rich people the least, but what can I do other than vote...and selfishly take advantage of the situation as a person who doesn't buy a lot of stuff.) My home state has chosen to get most of its tax revenues from consumers. Because I make a concerted and successful effort to consume relatively little, my tax burden here is quite low compared to what it would be in many other states. If I were the type of person who bought a lot of stuff, Tennessee might not be a good place to live because I'd be eaten alive by the high sales tax. But because of the way I'll be making and spending money going forward, I'm essentially under-taxed here.

The reason to worry about such complicated stuff is, of course, that further stretching of saved dollars can make a better life more affordable during retirement. The ultimate goal is maximum happiness, after all, and the realist understands that less money spent on expenses and taxes means more money available to fund a happy life. Money may not be able to buy happiness, but a certain amount of money is required to make happiness possible. It's a required element. Is it the only consideration, or even the most important one? Of course not. As humans, we also require certain combinations of fulfilling social interaction with people we enjoy, a climate and landscape that's a good match for our biological and spiritual make-up, and pleasing levels and types of privacy and peace and culture and excitement. So many factors come into play when one considers possible relocation and decides whether or not to say, "This place feels like it could be *home*."

As a couple of dudes who happen to have been born into a minority and are married to each other, and who in middle age require a certain level of social comfort, we know that we wouldn't be able to maintain maximum happiness in many low cost-of-living areas in the U.S. or in various other countries. We could buy a plot of land in rural Tennessee on the cheap and build a modest dream house and never run out of money, for instance, but we'd likely be surrounded by other humans who made us feel less than comfortable. (When I first announced I was moving to Nashville a friend said, "You do know that when you venture outside Nashville you're in Tennessee, right?" Once I got here and explored, I understood what she meant. Suffice to say that small-town culture in the American South doesn't offer a comfortable niche for minorities, and I'm too old to fight such a battle at this stage of life.) We're pretty darned happy right where we are, breathing easily in Nashville's little progressive bubble, enjoying access to an increasingly vibrant scene we can share with a chosen family of friends we absolutely love. We may stay right where we are.

But we're open to other options as well, including some that many would consider rather adventurous. We've looked at other areas of the U.S., and come across some that held serious allure when we visited. Dave is a massive fan of San Diego and we both love San Francisco, but cost of living in these cities is off the scale and we'd need to work like dogs until we expired to fund a decent life in these places (I'm not interested in such an existence). The same goes for Palm Springs, which is beautiful and very gay-friendly but seemed a bit too hot and dry and snooty. Northern New Mexico is gorgeous and had a really strong spiritual appeal for both of us, but something didn't quite click. The Outer Banks of North Carolina? Hurricanes and a nasty barrage of anti-gay legislation coming out of the state government. Chicago? Wonderful people and culture, but those winters! These are all wonderful places to visit, but along with many other U.S. spots they just don't feel like "home" options. And all have one big obstacle in common. They're all in the United States, where health care costs are astronomical and (until the system is fixed) getting worse. The U.S. has a relatively high cost of living overall, and once you throw our crazy health care costs into the mix...it's really expensive here. This will be an increasingly important concern as we age.

Politicians love to spit out the applause line, "America is the greatest nation in the world!" In many ways, this is certainly true. I, for one, am extremely grateful that I was born into many advantages not enjoyed by, say, the soul inhabiting the body of a newborn child in the dirty slums of Mumbai or the war-torn deserts of Libya. I experienced some challenges back in the day when I made $11,000 a year and sometimes dinner was a package of Ramen noodles, but I never had to worry about dying because I had *nothing* to eat or drink. I also never had to worry about being thrown in jail for stating an opinion, or losing my home because someone dropped a bomb on me. I know I'm fortunate, and I appreciate it fully. That said, I also know that my life is more than half over and I have options regarding how I live the rest of it. Even if the U.S. really is "the greatest nation," it's not the greatest in every category. We live on a big planet, and a lot of other countries offer as much or more in various respects and categories.

Just as American states provide different assortments of pros and cons that can fit into individual lives more or less nicely, so do other countries. And the differences are much more dramatic. Are the pros worth the cons? This is for the individual to decide. Health care in Costa Rica can cost half or a third of what it does in the U.S. and quality is good, but you may have to take a three-hour bus ride to get to the best facilities, or share a hospital room with seven other patients and bring your own toilet paper. An air-conditioned two-bedroom apartment overlooking the Rio Cuale in Puerto Vallarta, Mexico, may only run you $250/month, but there may be roosters living across the street and if your toilet stops working it may be a month before someone shows up to fix it. Dinner and drinks in Cuenca, Ecuador, can be yours for four bucks, but you may need to be fluent in Spanish if you want to figure out how to pay your electric bill when you don't have a mailbox.

Personally, I'm interested and intrigued. I stumbled upon the concept of expatriation kind of by accident, learning a bit online and then reading some great books by Americans who've successfully transitioned into really cool lives in interesting places (I'll recommend some of my favorites at the end of this book). At the very least, we've seen some awe-inspiring environments, met some wonderful new friends, and accumulated precious memories while visiting possible relocation spots. The relaxed, live-and-let-live feel of Latin America suits me, as does the clean humidity in mountainous regions where the rain forest meets the Pacific Ocean. And we could live comfortably on half as much money.

We love the small, gay-friendly, expat-populated town of Manuel Antonio on Costa Rica's central Pacific coast. Dave isn't sure there's enough culture or activity, but as soon as we made it to the coast and sat down for lunch in the mountains overlooking the sea I found myself in tears and unable to even speak. I remember thinking, "I feel like I was always meant to be here." Puerto Vallarta, Mexico, has a completely different type of appeal that hit me a bit more gradually. It would be an easier move (tens of thousands of American ex-pats already live there, and they have a freaking Home Depot and Costco), and the city is quite charming with its cobblestone streets and blend of grit and romance. I was shocked when we stopped at a street market to stock up on all the food two men could carry and our bill came to twelve dollars.

After two visits each, these two places have already achieved home-away-from-home status for us, and we'll likely return just for leisure if we're not continuing to investigate relocation. Before serious consideration, we'd want to stay in one spot for weeks and then months, then if we did relocate we'd rent for a while (rather than buying a place) or maybe permanently. I'd like to see more of these two countries, and I'm also semi-obsessed with diving a bit deeper and checking out Granada and San Juan del Sur in Nicaragua and perhaps some spots in Panama and Ecuador, the two countries that regularly appear at the very top of "best ex-pat destinations" lists. With a bit of Latin American travel planning under my belt, I can get us to and from these spots (with interesting and sometimes luxurious accommodations) for a song. I don't know if I'll ever be shopping for one-way tickets, but it remains a possibility. Should we ever make that choice, life will get complicated for a bit before it gets easier.

If moving from one city or state to another within the U.S. is a bit of work, moving to another country is an ordeal of epic proportions. Because this is a book about saving and investing for early retirement and not a book about moving to another country, I won't delve into the minutia. Just know that if you decide expatriation is an option you decide you find interesting, you'll have a ton of research ahead of you should you want to seriously consider it.

Moving to another country requires more than just packing your crap and getting on a plane.

Some ex-pats manage to live outside the U.S. for years and even permanently on a perpetual tourist visa. Basically, they leave their adopted country before each 90-day visa expires (or at some other interval specific to that country), then return after the required number of days, lather, rinse, repeat. Others who prefer to do things the official way (and not risk getting in trouble) jump through the hoops required to gain legal residency. Requirements vary wildly by country. Generally some proof of adequate and reliable permanent income is first on the list (these countries maintain social programs designed to keep their populations healthy, secure, and educated...they don't want immigrants coming into the country to sponge off of their governments any more than the U.S. does). Then they will need to see proof that you're healthy and not a criminal. Assorted documents may or may not need to be translated by an approved translator, and approved at an embassy in the U.S. or at some facility in some other part of the country to which you hope to reside. All the red tape can get stuck on itself for months or even a year or more, and it can cost a bit to get it unstuck.

In most other countries, it's likely that you won't be able to legally work if you're not drawing a paycheck working remotely for a U.S. employer. Just as the U.S. doesn't want undocumented immigrants taking jobs from Americans, these countries don't want you showing up and taking a job away from one of their residents. In many places, you can own a business and employ locals, but if you get caught drawing a paycheck doing work a local could do...enjoy being deported. Some countries will only allow you to purchase real estate if you have a certain type of residency; others don't care, while still others will only allow foreign citizens to buy property of certain types or in certain parts of the country. It's kind of like investing in the stock market; there is a *lot* to know, and you'll need to know a lot of it before you leap. (But the rewards can be pretty cool. If you want to live in a beautiful place that makes you happy and where a pineapple costs a quarter and you never have to worry about money again, maybe it's worth it.)

Interested in moving to a country in Europe? Be prepared to pay a very hefty fee to buy into the socialized health care plans in those countries. Their residents have been funding government-run health care all their lives, and you don't get to just show up and take advantage of the situation. Thinking about Australia or New Zealand? You'll need to prove that you have upwards of $700,000 in savings so they know you can afford to stay there.

That's probably more than enough said about relocation. Again, those interested in other countries in particular may enjoy the starting-point list of books, blogs, web sites, and Facebook pages at the end of this book. It's a sub-topic, and in my opinion even if it only leads to more adventurous (and cheaper) travel, the concept is worth a look. We're all about maximizing our resources, right? Why spend $2000 on a week in Orlando when you could spend $1000 for a massively-enriching adventure in Central America and invest the other $1000? That's what I say, anyway.

Regardless of where one chooses to settle for an extended post-working life phase, there's the pesky matter of...covering the expenses that life brings while never running out of money. Let's talk about how we'll accomplish this.

A recent Gallup poll indicates that about half of Americans worry that they won't be able to afford retirement at all, and may need to work until death to cover the expenses of living. This sounds awful, and I know that if I hadn't looked at the road ahead and made some dramatic changes I could easily have been one of these people. Because I started by taking care of my later years first, ensuring that I had investments in place to cover those traditional retirement years before methodically working my way back to the present before declaring myself financially independent, I have no fear of running out of money. If I thought there was any chance I'd end up a broken and penniless retirement failure, I'd keep working. The peace of mind is wonderful! But I do want to be sure I withdraw my dollars strategically once it's time to begin living off of investments. The more efficiently I handle my post-retirement finances, the more options I'll have as I enjoy my freedom. Fortunately others have blazed a trail, and there are simple guidelines we can all follow. Individual circumstances may require flexibility, of course.

Hit the 401k (and/or traditional IRA) last. It's a good (okay, great) idea to leave tax-advantaged accounts alone as long as possible. By the time one turns 59 ½ and can begin withdrawing money from a 401k account without worrying about penalties or complicated strategies required to avoid them, there's a lot of never-taxed money sitting there earning more money. We want to let this nice situation continue as long as we can, right? The tax man requires that we begin withdrawing money from 401k accounts and traditional IRAs the year we turn 70 ½. If we can wait until then, or at least wait as long as possible, we maximize our earnings. We like maximizing, so the goal should be to let the 401k sit peacefully and pleasantly where it is for as long as we can.

Hit the Roth IRA second-last. We've discussed the beauty of the Roth IRA; our investment earnings in this vehicle are never subject to taxes. Another fabulous feature of the Roth is that there is *no* requirement that we begin taking money out of it, at any age. If we choose, we can leave our Roth investments where they are until we're dead, and in most cases our heirs won't have to pay taxes on the earnings either. This is pretty great! While there will eventually be years when pulling out some tax-free earnings will makes sense (in combination with other withdrawals that are subject to taxes), I personally love the idea of earning as much tax-free dough as possible in my Roth IRA. Generally, I like considering this the place to hit second-last to fund retirement.

Plan to leave tax-advantaged retirement accounts untouched for as long as practically and legally possible.

During the first years of my own post-work life, I'll be covering some of our household expenses with limited income from random ventures, my cash stockpile, and a portion of my taxable investment account's dividend income that isn't being automatically reinvested in index funds. At some point, probably after Dave has stopped working too, we'll eventually hit the day when it's time to begin selling investments in both of our taxable accounts. This will be a little sad, because I so enjoy watching the account balances grow. But...this is why we put the money there in the first place! Once the accumulation phase ends, it's time to quit working and wisely use that money to fund a great life. Yeah, baby!

Hit the taxable investment account first, in combination with savings and other income. Those who've stuck with just index funds (and/or other mutual funds) will just begin selling shares in those funds as the money is needed, and the process will be fairly simple. Some experts recommend pulling out a year's total all at once and keeping it in a low-interest money market fund throughout the year, to avoid worries of stock market turbulence. Others go with a withdraw-it-as-you-need-it strategy. I plan to land somewhere in-between these concepts, depending on how the stock market is looking at the time. But remember that timing the market is generally as thankless a task when taking money *out* as it is when buying stock on the front end. So you should probably forget that I just told you about my plan. For the average early retiree, I'd recommend withdrawing a few months' supply of cash at a time, keeping track of the total amount budgeted for that year and not exceeding it.

Those who've joined me in the world of investing in individual stocks will have more thinking to do when selling taxable investments. It'll be all about keeping the stocks most likely to perform the best going forward as long as possible, and selling the stocks with less potential first. Transaction fees will come into play, so selling large chunks of each stock at once may be a good idea to minimize those fees. Current dividend yield of each stock will need to be considered as well. And from the semi-advanced category...if you're going to be taking a capital gain on a stock sale, it can be smart to see if you have any dogs in the portfolio that you can sell during the same tax year to take a tax loss harvest. This complicated strategy is best explained with an example.

Tax Loss Harvest Digression for the Semi-Advanced

Let's say it's the year 2025 and I'm selling some shares in Stock A. This stock has done well for me, and has gone up $5,000 since I bought it. If my overall income is at a certain level, I may get hit with capital gains taxes on this profit. But...I also happen to have some crappy shares in Stock B that I can sell at the same time. This stock has been a stinker, and has gone down $3,000 since I bought it. I just want to get what money I still have out of there, so I sell. The good news is that my $3,000 loss on Stock B goes against my $5,000 gain on Stock A, and I'll end up only owing capital gains tax on $2,000 of my profit on that Stock A. Since I was going to end up unloading Stock B anyway, I was smart to sell it the same year I was also going to register some capital gains. I "harvested" my tax loss.

But I digress! Where were we? Ah yes, figuring out the order for account withdrawals in retirement.

Basically, we'll want to hit our taxable account first and try to save our tax-advantaged accounts for later. Keeping an eye on any additional income during each tax year and the total of capital gains and dividend income in that same year is a good idea. If we get close to jumping into a higher tax bracket, we can consider scaling back expenses a bit or drawing on any cash stashed in savings or checking accounts, etc., to avoid showing excessive income until the next tax year. (You can just file the last few sentences in the back of your brain, and once you're living off of your investments it will make more sense! No need to pay extra taxes, you know.)

There's one important reminder that belongs right here.

Remember, always, that you're still following a plan that began when you first started plotting to retire early. Stick to it.

If you went with a 4% safe withdrawal rate, your total withdrawals in year one should be no more than 4% of your cash/investment total at the beginning of that year. If you went with 3% or 5%, that's what you get. Adjust annually for inflation. Keep an eye on the plan and feel free to adjust as needed. And never panic if the market temporarily drops (don't sell low) or go crazy if the market rallies (don't overspend when caught up in market euphoria). Think long-term. Stick to the plan. Remain calm, happy, and retired.

WRAP-UP

Have you made it all the way to the conclusion of this book? If so, congratulations! As you well know, I get a little excited about some of these saving and investment topics and can't stop talking about the details once I get started. I hope I haven't rambled *too* much. Because really, my plan is more about the generalities than the specifics. It's about starting with a basic, rather casual mindset and letting a general goal turn into success and a better life. We meet here at the end of a bunch of chapters in my own story as the rest are about to be written, and hopefully at the beginning of some chapters of *yours* that are about to be revised for the better.

Should you care to join me in the relatively small (but growing) community of those who took a good look at life the way it was and decided to stealthily adjust the present to create a future of freedom, please do! I'm telling the truth when I say that compared to surviving the last few years of working (which was a rather monumental feat), getting to this place of comfort really wasn't all that difficult. And the reason was that I never considered money my goal, rather a tool I'd need to reach my true goal of happiness. I thought about changing the job I had or switching to a new one, but decided to go for the big prize and changed my mindset instead. I wanted that permanent solution. I chose financial freedom, and figured out how to get it.

The specifics were a bit daunting at first, but not once I educated myself. The hard part was accomplishing my own personal buy-in of the generalities on the front end. Do you want to work for The Man for the rest of your life, or for most of it? No? Then hire yourself to work a second job concurrently with the one you already have. This new job is you working for your future self, gradually building a different and better way of life. Put your heart and soul into this new second job, and you'll find that it's easy because you really *love* working for your future self!

If *any* item or experience you're thinking about purchasing (even if it costs almost nothing) isn't going to enhance your life more than achieving financial freedom sooner, direct the money you were going to spend into debt pay-off and creation of a sensible emergency fund, then into your investments and your future. Don't deny yourself all fun and pleasure, just the stuff that isn't as pleasing as making financial progress. As you begin to gain ground, you'll find that financial progress is quite fun and pleasing. Celebrate each new lifestyle change that adds financial efficiency to your existence! Enjoy the search for increased life enjoyment at a lower price! And thanks to the power of compounding and the magic of the stock market going up and down and ultimately up, progress increasingly builds upon itself and saved money turns itself into more money.

Live well, but live sensibly and with your long-term goal in mind. If you don't care to spend a lot of time learning about investing, no problem! You can stick to index funds and do better than 80% of the goofballs who manage stock portfolios for a living. If you care to fine-tune your strategies later and dig further into the nuances of the stock market, you can. If you don't care to do this, just work a little longer and don't worry about it. What's going to make you happier in a big-picture sense? That's what you'll want to do. That's what this book is all about, after all. We want to live a good life now, and a better and ridiculously great life later. Let's have it all, shall we?

It's Sunday afternoon. As I type these last thoughts before declaring the rough draft of this book (created on a half-price reconditioned laptop I found on eBay) finished, I'm preparing to walk into my small-but-efficient kitchen and pour myself a glass of filtered tap water. I'll then step out onto the deck of my modest, just-large-enough-for-two-people-and-a-cat house (where the summer thermostat is set at 76) and look out at the yard I mow myself in my unassuming, inexpensive neighborhood. Later I'll throw on an old pair of cheap shorts and a T-shirt I got for free and take my 15-year-old paid-off vehicle to Aldi, where I'll use my cash-back-bonus credit card to spend about $25 for fresh food items that will last us most of the week when I incorporate staples bought in bulk at Costco and cook meals at home. Then Dave and I will sit and stream a movie or watch free digital broadcast television and not miss cable TV for a second, and eventually we'll head to bed to sleep on the like-new mattress a friend gave us because she didn't have room for it in her house. I'll set the alarm on my years-out-of-date cell phone that still works just fine, and wake before the alarm even goes off in the morning because I'll want to check my stocks and read a few articles that might help me fine-tune my investment strategy. Then I'll head up to work, where the stress will be unbelievable and I'll be hating every minute until I stop and realize that this last part, the part about working, is just about finished.

And then I'll stop for a moment and smile. Because several years ago I decided to get casually serious about how I was living so that I could create a better, wonderful future free of the need to suffer for a paycheck. And I did it. I won. I'm the guy who never got paid much and is about to shock the world by retiring early. It's almost time for me to make that phone call to the boss and say, "You may want to brace yourself. I'm calling to discuss the details of my impending retirement." Wow. That's going to be kind of fun! It was epic, the battle of me against The Man. But it's over now.

I kicked his ass.

AFTERWARD: THE LISTS!

50 Money-Saving Ideas

Here's a whole slew of money-saving ideas either employed successfully at our house or recommended by so many friends and acquaintances in online communities that I felt like I had to include them in this book somewhere. My plan involves a mindset shift more than specifics, but maybe some of these will help get your juices flowing.

1. Make your own food! Bread, salad dressing, marinara sauce, soup, pizza including the sauce and crust, meals in general...if it was prepared and/or packaged, you paid someone to do something you might have been able to do (better) on your own. A pot of homemade soup gives you 7-8 servings for the same price as a single-serving can of soup bought at the grocery store (and tastes better).

2. If you're still paying for cable or satellite TV in this day and age...why?

3. If you smoke cigarettes, consider quitting, cutting way back, or moving to the Philippines or Indonesia where they cost 50 cents a pack and you can smoke under a palm tree.

4. Filter your own water and don't fall for one of the biggest scams ever: bottled American water.

5. Combine errands, rather than getting in the car to do just one thing before driving back home. Even when gas isn't outrageous, it's expensive.

6. Don't overpay for cell phone service. There are great low-cost options available these days (consider taking your existing phone to Cricket, all-in for $35 per month with auto-pay). When updating a phone (only when truly necessary), avoid installment plans. And if you're one of the few who still has a land line, ask yourself why.

7. Don't buy gifts for holidays just because some commercial said it's what you're supposed to do.

8. Try adjusting your thermostat up a degree or two during summer and down a degree or two during winter. If you don't notice, try another degree or two.

9. Don't assume clothes need to go into the laundry after one wearing.

10. Consider international travel, especially to low-cost-of-living countries. You may find that a little research and a little courage can result in a cheaper and more enriching experience beyond our borders.

11. If planning to park at the airport for more than a few days, consider taking Lyft or Uber (or asking a friend to drive you). A car service to-and-from may cost less than parking.

12. If your peer group likes nights on the town, organize a BYOB pot-luck gathering at your house (everybody brings their own drinks and a dish to share) and see if it catches on with the group. You may end up having more fun for way less money.

13. Sell your old crap on eBay. Some sucker out there probably wants it.

14. Check out Costco, Aldi, Trader Joe's, the local Latino market...find bargains and stock up on them. Different stores present different saving opportunities. Don't get stuck on particular brand names.

15. Be sure you need or are getting sufficient benefit from any prescription or over-the-counter drugs you purchase regularly.

16. Mow your own lawn and trim your own shrubs.

17. Clean your own house and wash your own vehicle.

18. Once you know you have the self-control to pay off the balance in full every month without fail, pay monthly bills with a cash-back credit card. Every so often you can move the rewards to your checking account, then into your investments.

19. Consider replacing expensive hobbies and leisure activities with less-expensive alternatives that might provide the same amount of pleasure.

20. If you won't be in a room for the next 30 seconds, turn off the light.

21. Don't heat or cool your home excessively during periods when everyone who lives there is asleep or not there.

22. Expensive jewelry is probably not necessary. Jewelry in general is suspect, especially if there's a lot of it in one person's possession.

23. For men in particular, consider a hairstyle that can be maintained at home without the need for a professional cut.

24. Install dimmer switches in your home for more stylish mood lighting and energy savings. If you don't know how to install a dimmer switch, ask a gay friend. We are notorious for installing dimmer switches the day we move into a new house.

25. Make extra portions of dinner and take the leftovers to work for lunch the next day. $10 per day for lunch is $200 per month, more than cable TV or smoking cigs or most monthly utility bill totals.

26. Try boxed wine. The stigma is outdated. I've bought boxed wine in Tuscany, for goodness sake.

27. If you need new glasses, comparison shop and stay out of the mall. (I had a great experience at America's Best. A true bargain on a solid product. $69 for two stylish frames with lenses, and a free eye exam. Saved hundreds versus the mall shops.) Skip the anti-glare coating. Consider using your existing prescription at an online glasses web site (be sure you have the pupil-distance measurement).

28. Think twice before habitually attending pro sporting events and paying $10-plus for a beer, who-knows-what for parking, etc. Pro team season tickets can be considered a major investment for which you will end up working noticeably longer.

29. Try to always be open to a less-expensive alternative. Maybe you'll end up liking the Costco toilet paper better than Charmin (I do!).

30. Would you rather see that movie at a theatre the weekend it's released, or stream it on TV next year when it's free?

31. Consider making oft-used products yourself. Money-saving instructions for creating many household cleaning products can be found with a simple online search.

32. Shred your own cheese to save money, enjoy a fresher and better-tasting product, and avoid eating cellulose (wood pulp, which can't be digested by the human body and is added to most shredded cheese).

33. Don't buy fireworks.

34. Rather than consuming, try creating.

35. Consider renting rather than buying items that won't be used often (possible examples: a chain saw, a pressure washer, a big truck).

36. If you're nursing an old, low-mileage vehicle, consider renting a car for long road trips. Just the savings on gas may pay for the rental, without considering wear and tear on your old clunker.

37. Gals, don't paint your nails when nobody is going to see them. If you're only going to see people who won't notice, don't paint them then either. (This concept can be extended to cosmetics in general.)

38. If you haven't eaten meat for at least a year or two, try going without deodorant to find out if you really still need it all the time. (Seriously! I only wear the stuff a few times a year, and a survey of people I know indicates that I don't stink. I hope they're telling the truth.)

39. If you're a cook, grow your own fresh herbs. In the right climate, with the right yard, consider planting a vegetable garden.

40. Plan meals based on low-price sale items and loss leaders available at the grocery store that week. Shopping without a list and instead planning meals around what's on sale can save lots of money. Clip coupons only for items you were going to buy anyway.

41. Make it your quest to stop bringing "stuff" into your house, instead working to get it out of there so you have more space in which you can exist. You may eventually find that you need less space. If your hobby is collecting something (anything), get over it and sell that crap on eBay.

42. Think about items you use often, and consider alternatives that are a better value. I switched from Edge shave gel to Trader Joe's mango shave cream, started picking up a year's supply when I drive across town to TJ's, and cut my shaving cream expense by 90% (it goes much further and works better, and for a guy who shaves his head this is a nice money-saver!).

43. Colored, flavored, carbonated water packaged as "Coke" or "Pepsi" might be nicely replaced by filtered water flavored with a slice of lemon or a fresh raspberry.

44. If you saw it on a TV commercial, you probably don't need it.

45. No law requires you to order a beverage other than free water when you're out to dinner.

46. Don't consider shopping a leisure activity. Shop to satisfy real needs, not for recreation.

47. It's likely that nobody needs to buy another bottle of perfume or cologne, even if they don't presently own any. It's also likely that nobody needs to buy a $40 bottle of scented water in a pretty box as a gift.

48. Kids are expensive! If you have kids, know that eventually they will leave the nest and a quick financial catch-up will be more than possible. I don't have kids, but in

less than ten years I went from a net worth close to zero to retirement. You'll be able to get there once you can really start saving.

49. You don't need that shirt. Put it back on the rack.

50. Will the item or experience you're about to buy enhance your life more than achieving financial independence earlier? Yes? Then go ahead and buy it! Surprise! Number 50 was a gimme!

Shop Your Way to Financial Independence: Shopping "Switches"

Obviously the best way to save money is to not spend it at all. But we can't go through life spending absolutely nothing, lest we end up dead of starvation or at least somewhat sad because we've deprived ourselves of all pleasure. Can we spend less for the same amount of pleasure? Certainly! Here are some random examples of this mindset translating into new, more-efficient purchasing habits. Some make a small difference, some a larger difference. When these "switches" become consistent, we end up with hundreds upon hundreds of extra dollars every year (and need hundreds of dollars per year less to live going forward).

Coffee. Switch from Starbucks to Aldi Honduran (good) or Costco bulk (great).
Clothes. Switch from Macy's to Kohl's on sale (good) or Goodwill (great).
Lunch. Switch from Subway to brown-bag sandwiches (good) or leftovers (great).
Transport. Switch from cabs to Lyft/Uber (good) or bikes/public transit (great).
Sports. Switch from NFL tickets to sports bar (good) or watch party (great).
Pizza. Switch from delivery to carry-out (good) or make it yourself (great).

Recreation. Switch from Disneyland to local carnival (good) or hiking trip (great).

Music. Switch from superstar concerts to CDs (good) or free local shows (great).

Movies. Switch from the cinema to DVD night (good) or streaming (great).

Learning. Switch from Rosetta Stone to Babbel (good) or Duolingo (great).

Vacation. Switch from Australia to Costa Rica (great) or Mexico (also great).

Phones. Switch from newest iPhone to previous model (good) or just wait (great).

Toys. Switch from Apple iPad to Amazon tablet (good) or existing phone (great).

Paying. Switch from cash to a cash-back credit card (great, but don't carry a balance, ever!)

Ten Food Items to Prepare Yourself

There's no need to buy many grocery items in a can or a box when you can, quickly and with very little trouble, prepare better-tasting, healthier, less expensive versions in your kitchen. Just google recipes or look at the ingredient list on a prepared and/or processed item's package (and remove the preservatives and other artificial crap!), and stop wasting money paying someone to plop out these products in a factory.

1. Bread/Pizza Dough
2. Pasta Sauces (marinara and pesto are super-easy)
3. Salsa/Guacamole
4. Vegetable Soup
5. Pancake/Waffle Mix
6. Chili
7. Pot Pies

8. Ice Cream (we use coconut milk in a cheap Cuisinart...amazing!)
9. Hummus
10. Cakes/Cookies/Quick Breads

Fun Things to Do When the Market Dips, Corrects, or Crashes

The sky is falling! The sky is falling! Okay, no, it isn't. The market goes up and down, and every now and then it goes down a lot. Don't worry about it! It's fun when investments explode to the upside, and it's sad when they drop like anchors. But in all cases, we must remember that we're in this for the long haul. You can remain calm, expect more than a century of market history to hold, and look forward to long-term gains if you're investing properly and using the following list as a guide during periods of massive market turbulence. While the market is dropping and all the uninformed, reactionary goofballs are selling, try some of these fun ideas:

1. Relax with a good book or movie, and perhaps a nice cocktail.
2. Twiddle your thumbs (i.e., do nothing).
3. Feel sorry for sellers turning paper losses into actual losses.
4. Repeat aloud: "The market always recovers and then goes higher."
5. Remember that your invested money is for the future, not that afternoon.
6. Congratulate yourself for being smart and not selling at market bottom.
7. Buy stocks while they're on sale.
8. Hold more cash or pay extra on your mortgage until things stabilize.
9. Google "100 year stock market graph," then see #4 above.

10. Smack yourself in the face if you even think about selling any stocks.

Dividend Aristocrats

Companies in the S&P 500 that have increased their dividend for at least the last 25 years, every year without fail, are known as the *Dividend Aristocrats*. For the buy-and-hold investor, a dividend increase is like a pay raise. If we buy our shares once and hold them for many years, every increase in our dividend really is great news. Perform your own Google search to get a list of Dividend Aristocrats as of the current year. This way you'll get up-to-date information, including current dividend percentage ("yield") for each Aristocrat. Also consider looking at a list of *Dividend Achievers* (companies that have increased dividends for at least ten consecutive years). I think it's worth considering investing in some of these if you, like me, decide to invest in some individual company stocks that will be bought and then held for a very long time.

The Basic Plan's Ten Essentials

There's a pretty huge cauldron of information behind you at this point, if you've survived all of this book. Perhaps a quick boil-down to major strategy highlights will be helpful!

1. **Drastically cut spending** by eliminating all non-life-enhancing expenses (while still enjoying life).
2. **Eliminate all disastrous debt** costing 5% or more.
3. **Build an emergency fund**.
4. **Prioritize workplace 401k** (max if possible/sensible), for later retirement years. S&P 500 index fund and/or total market index fund recommended.
5. **Consider an HSA** over traditional health insurance, if available.

6. **Fund a Roth IRA**, for middle retirement years and beyond. S&P 500 index fund and/or safe dividend growth stocks recommended.

7. **Direct all remaining saved cash into a taxable investment account**, for early retirement years and beyond. S&P 500 index fund and/or total market index fund recommended. Tread carefully and with purpose if deciding to build an additional portfolio of individual company stocks.

8. When the cash/investment stockpile exceeds 20-25 times anticipated year-one living expenses during retirement, **declare financial independence**.

9. **Enjoy life**, filling any early post-working-years void with enjoyable activities and adventures planned in advance.

10. **Keep an eye on your finances** and withdraw funds from accounts strategically. Monitor investments, adjust/rebalance as needed, learn about account conversions and rollovers and tax efficiency (once you have time on your hands because you beat The Man, you can google this stuff!).

References and Inspirations

The Complete Idiot's Guide to Retiring Early by Dee Lee and Jim Flewelling (book). Some of the information here is very out of date (the book was published in 2001), but the basics are covered nicely. A lot has changed since the authors compiled their info (bonds, inflation, health care…all much different now), but I still recommend this one for a great introduction to basics and for general reference.

Early Retirement Extreme by Jacob Lund Fisker (book). This one is a difficult and challenging read, in a tone kind of like a text book, but great as encouragement for a philosophical shift. This guy (a well-known figure among those who are part of the early retirement movement) is hard-core, but offers a lot of specific advice of use to anyone ready to get serious about major changes. There's also an exhaustive supply of great, detailed information at **www.earlyretirementextreme.com**.

Mr. Money Mustache (web site and blog). The popular site **www.mrmoneymustache.com** is truly a must-visit destination. Colorado resident and former Canadian Pete Adeney may presently be the top figure in the early retirement movement, with good reason. His advice regarding "achieving financial freedom through badassity" is entertaining and infinitely useful. I recommend starting at his first blog entry and reading straight through to the end (which will take weeks or months). The forums on the site are nicely organized and full of great stories and tips from many members of a growing online community. Become a fan of the not-officially-affiliated Facebook pages *Mustachians on Facebook* and *Mustachians in Practice* for constant motivation and helpful tips from like-minded individuals.

The Millionaire Next Door by Thomas J. Stanley and William D. Danko (book). This is one of the classics, perhaps *the* classic, on the topic of adjusting lifestyle and spending in order to amass a surprisingly huge nest egg.

The Mad Fientist (web site) offers lots of great concepts and strategies, especially for those interested in obsessing over optimization and specific numbers. The idea here is to take a "scientific" approach to achieving financial independence, or F.I. (Thus the clever spin on the word "scientist," converting it to F.I.-entist.) This is a great place to start when looking for answers regarding taxes and how to minimize them. There's also a popular podcast. **www.madfientist.com**.

Retirement without Borders by Barry Golson with Thia Golson (book). This one is a nice overview of overseas retirement as a concept, and covers a bunch of warm-climate options in great detail. It includes testimonials and tips from ex-pats who actually live in various locales and share good and bad personal experiences. It was published in 2008, so some of the specifics are getting a bit out-of-date. A fun read.

The *Happier than a Billionaire* series by Nadine Hays Pisani (book). Now a longtime Facebook friend of mine, Nadine covers the first-hand ins and hilarious outs of moving to Costa Rica in three highly entertaining books. There's also a blog at her web site **www.happierthanabillionaire.com** and a fun Facebook page (become a fan for great pictures and entertaining updates). The real-life adventures of Nadine and her husband Rob inspired my tune "Pura Vida (Pure Life)." You can check out a goofy video Dave and I filmed for this song while vacationing in Costa Rica here: **https://youtu.be/qnljO5BKu08**.

Go Curry Cracker (web site and blog). These young nomads quit working in their thirties to start a family and travel the world. Their mantra is, "Spend little, save more, travel the world. Go curry cracker!" Don't be misled by the cute saying and web site moniker; these people have done serious research and put it into action. This is a great place to learn about not just lifestyle adjustment but also complicated stuff like strategically rolling retirement funds into a Roth IRA to minimize or eliminate taxes. They also maintain a nice Facebook page. **www.gocurrycracker.com**

Tieland to Thailand (web site and blog). This photogenic young American couple quit working and bought one-way tickets to Chiang Mai, Thailand. They share fun stories of their lifestyle evolution on the blog and also on an enjoyable Facebook page. **www.tielandtothailand.com**.

The Minimalists (web site and blog). Joshua Fields Millburn and Ryan Nicodemus have built a following of millions, sharing inspirational tales of creating more meaningful lives after stripping out the unnecessary clutter. I enjoy following their Facebook page, and often find that they post a bit of philosophy or a link to a great article or blog post just when I most need some motivation. **www.theminimalists.com**.

Investing and Personal Finance Club (Facebook group). This is a friendly and well-moderated Facebook community, made up of retail investors at every experience level. It's a good place to go for random advice or to just monitor the questions and answers coming from others trying to improve their investing skills.

Dividend Growth Investing (Facebook group). This is another Facebook community, suitable for those interested in various perspectives from investors going beyond mutual funds to increase dividend income. Some members of this group give good advice, while others most definitely do not.

Google (web search engine). Day or night, you can always go to **www.google.com** and google random questions to see where the effort leads you. The answers are probably out there somewhere, you know. I googled "how can I retire early" a number of years ago and it led me, ultimately, to financial independence!

Made in the USA
San Bernardino, CA
21 March 2017